Our Best Ever Ulster Cook Book

Our Best Ever Ulster Cook Book
© Copyright Causeway Press, September 2010

Published by

Printed by

jcprint ltd
BELFAST

Telephone 07860 205333
Fax 029 9079 0420
email: info@jcprint.net

Contents

Conversion Tables

Weight

Metric	Imperial
25 gms	1 oz
50 gms	2 oz
75 gms	3 oz
100 gms	4 oz/¼ lb
125 gms	-5 oz
150 gms	+5 oz
175 gms	6 oz
200 gms	7 oz
225 gms	8 oz/½ lb
250 gms	9 oz
275 gms	10 oz
300 gms	11 oz
325 gms	-12 oz/¾ lb
350 gms	+ 12 oz
375 gms	13 ozs
400 gms	14 oz
425 gms	15 oz
450 gms	16 oz/1 lb
675 gms	22 oz/½ lb
1 kgs	2.2 lb
1.2 kgs	2½ lb
1.3 kgs	3 lbs
1.8 kgs	4 lbs
2.2 kgs	5 lbs

Volume

Metric	Imperial
5 mls	1tsp
10 mls	1 dsp
15 mls	3 tsp/1 tblsp/½ fl oz
30 mls	2 tblsp/1 fl oz
60 mls	2 fl oz
90 mls	3 fl oz
120 mls	4 fl oz
150 mls	5 fl oz/¼ pt
180 mls	6 fl oz
210 mls	7 fl oz
240 mls	8 fl oz
270 mls	9 fl oz
300 mls	10 fl oz/½ pt
330 mls	11 fl oz
360 mls	12 fl oz
390 mls	13 fl oz
420 mls	14 fl oz
450 mls	15 fl oz/¾ pt
480 mls	16 fl oz
600 mls	20 fl oz/1 pt
960 mls	32 fl oz
1.1 ltr	40 fl oz/2 pt

Temperature

°C	°F	Gas Mark	Heat
110	225	¼	very cool
130	250	½	
140	275	1	cool
150	300	2	
170	325	3	moderate
180	350	5	
190	375	5	moderately hot
200	400	6	
220	425	7	hot
230	450	8	
240	475	9	very hot

Bread & Scones

Cherry & Fruit Scones

½ lb soda bread flour	½ tsp salt
2 oz margarine	2 oz castor sugar
1 egg	4 tbs milk
2 oz cherries (chopped)	2 oz sultanas

Sift flour into a bowl, rub in margarine and add castor sugar. Add cherries and sultanas, bind together with egg, add milk to make a firm but pliable dough, knead until smooth. Roll out three quarters inch thick cut out with a two inch cutter, can be plain or fluted. Place on greased baking tray, bake 10-12 minutes. Cool by placing a damp tea towel over hot scones. This prevents the tops being hard.
Freezable - Remove from freezer 2-3 hours before use or defrost in microwave.

Fruity Rock Buns

8 oz self raising flour	½ tsp baking powder
4 oz margarine	3 oz castor sugar
1 oz mixed peel	4 ox mixed fruit
2 eggs	1 tbsp milk

Place all the ingredients in a mixing bowl and beat together for 2-3 minutes. Place a heaped teaspoon of the mixture well apart on a baking tray previously brushed with margarine. Bake in a pre-heated oven at Gas 4, 400°F on second shelf from the top for 15-20 minutes.

Wheaten Bread

6 oz plain flour	2 oz margarine
10 oz wheat meal	1 egg
1 oz castor sugar	buttermilk
2 level tsp salt	2 level tsp baking soda
1 level tsp cream of tartar	

Rub margarine into flour and wheatmeal, add all dry ingredients. Make dough fairly soft, put into greased loaf tin. Bake at 375-400°F or gas 6-7.

Soda Scones

10 oz soda flour	4 oz sultanas
3 oz margarine	buttermilk
3 oz sugar	

Rub margarine into flour, add sugar and sultanas, mix with a little buttermilk until a stiff dough. Press on a floured board until half an inch thick, cut into rings and place on a baking tray. Bake in hot oven, 200°C for 10-15 minutes.

Tea Time Scones

12 oz self raising flour
4 oz butter or margarine
1 egg

pinch of salt
3 oz castor sugar
milk to mix

Place all the ingredients in a mixing bowl and beat together for 2-3 minutes. Place a heaped teaspoon of the mixture well apart on a baking tray previously brushed with margarine. Bake in a pre-heated oven at Gas 4, 400°F on second shelf from the top for 15-20 minutes.

Sweet Milk Scones

12 oz self raising flour
2 oz sugar
little milk

2 oz margarine
1 egg
pinch of salt

Rub margarine into flour, salt and sugar. Form soft dough with beaten egg to which enough milk has been added to make a teacup full. Turn on to floured board, knead lightly, roll out to half inch thick and cut into small rounds. Bake on greased trays at 500°F, 250°C, for 8-10 minutes or 10-15 minutes at 425°F.

Pancakes

1 lb soda bread flour
1 tbsp syrup
buttermilk to mix

5 oz sugar
2 eggs

Sieve flour and sugar. Add syrup, beaten eggs and enough buttermilk to make a dropping consistency. Drop spoonfuls on to a hot pan or griddle.

Sweet Scones

1 lb self raising soda bread flour
4 oz margarine

2 oz castor sugar
½ pint sweet milk

Pre heat oven to 220°C (top shelf), grease a baking sheet. Sieve flour into a bowl, stir in the sugar. Rub in margarine until mixture is crumbly (fruit may be added at this stage if desired). Add milk and mix to a soft dough. Roll out on to a floured board to half inch thickness. Cut into rounds with a two inch cutter. Place on a baking sheet and cook for 15-20 minutes until well risen and brown. Cool on a wire tray.

Pancakes

8 oz self raising soda bread flour
½ pint milk

3 oz castor sugar
1 egg

Sieve flour and sugar, add beaten egg, mix quickly into a batter adding buttermilk gradually. Pour into a large jug and pour out small quantities on to a well greased heated griddle. Turn when heat bubbles burst on top side. Heat griddle before you begin to mix and mix lightly and quickly.

Cakes

Quick Fruit Loaf

8 oz (225 g) self raising flour
2 oz (50 g) sugar
2 oz (50 g) fruit

1 egg
1 cup of milk
4 oz (100 g) margarine

Put flour, sugar and salt into a basin. Add melted margarine and mix all together. Put in a greased and floured tin and bake for 45 minutes at 350°F.

Farmhouse Loaf Cake

6 oz (175 g) self raising flour
5 oz (150 g) margarine
5 oz (150 g) castor sugar
2 eggs

2 Cadbury flakes
2 oz (50 g) cherries
3 oz (75 g) ground almonds

Cream margarine and sugar. Crumble chocolate flake and add flour, cherries and ground almonds plus eggs. Bake in a 2 lb loaf tin at 350°F until firm.

Almond & Cherry Cake

8 oz butter
8 oz sugar
8 oz plain flour
½ tsp baking powder

4 oz ground almonds
4 oz cherries (halved)
3 eggs

Cream butter and sugar. Beat eggs. Sift flour and baking powder. Add eggs and flour to creamed mixture. Stir in almonds and cherries. Bake in a slow oven for 2 hours 30 minutes.

Harvest Loaf

4 oz soft margarine
4 oz castor sugar
2 eggs
½ pt milk less 2 tblsps

12 oz mixed fruit
8 oz self raising flour
1 level tsp mixed spice

Put all ingredients into a bowl. Beat until well mixed 4-5 minutes. Pour into a greased 2 lb loaf tin. Bake at 325°F or gas mark 3 for one and a half to one and three quarter hours. Leave in tin for ten minutes before turning out. (note - the last five ingredients are optional and variable)

Banana Loaf

2 ripe bananas
4 oz soft margarine
6 oz castor sugar
8 oz self raising flour

2 large eggs
1 level tsp baking powder
2 tblsp milk

Put bananas into a bowl. Switch beater on and leave to mash, then add all the ingredients and mix for ten seconds. Put into prepared loaf tin, and bake in the centre of the oven for one and a quarter hours until well risen and golden brown. Gas 4 or 350ºF.

Rich Celebration/Christmas Cake

8 oz (200 g) butter
8 oz (200 g) sugar
8 oz (200 g) flour
4 medium sized eggs
8 oz (200 g) currants
8 oz (200 g) raisins
3 oz (75 g) cherries
3 oz (75 g) almonds
grated rind and juice of one lemon

1 tbsp (15 ml) brandy or brown sherry or milk
½ tsp (2.5 g) mixed spice
¼ tsp (1.25 g) cinnamon
a good pinch of ground cloves
1 tbsp (15 ml) of black treacle

* note the last five ingredients are optional and variable.

Sieve the flour and dust about a quarter of the flour over the prepared fruit. (The fruit should be prepared the night before baking and, if sherry or brandy is used, this should be spooned over the fruit in a clean bowl to allow it to soak overnight). Mix lightly until the fruit is well covered with flour. Beat the butter until it is soft, then add the sugar gradually. Beat until the grains of sugar have disappeared and the mixture is light and fluffy. If used, the treacle should be beaten into the creamed butter and sugar. Add the whole eggs, one at a time, adding a little of the flour should the mixture show signs of curdling. Sieve the spices, if used, into the remaining flour and stir the flour into the mixture, adding the lemon juice and rind, the milk (if used) and lastly stir in the fruit, the almonds (the 3 oz [75 g]) can be all coarsely chopped almonds or a mixture of 2 oz (50 g) ground almonds and 1 oz (25 g) coarsely chopped almonds) and the cherries (lightly tossed in flour). Mix well. Spoon the mixture into the prepared tin, spreading it up a little at the sides and leaving the centre hollow. Bake in a slow moderate oven, 325ºF for 3 ½- 4 hours, lowering the heat to slow 275ºF after the first 1/2 hours. If the top of the cake is becoming too brown during cooking, cover lightly with greaseproof or brown paper. When cooked, remove from oven and leave to cool in the tin before turning out.

Delicious Fruit Cake

12 oz Neill's Golden Fleece plain flour
8 oz castor sugar
8 oz mixed currants and sultanas
4 oz glace cherries
¼ tsp salt
1 level tsp baking powder

8 oz butter or margarine
4 large eggs
8 oz seedless raisins
150 ml brandy or milk
½ tsp mixed spice
grated rind of one lemon

Grease and line a nine inch cake tin. Cream fat and sugar and add beaten eggs a little at a time. Fold in sieved dry ingredients adding alternatively with dried fruit. Add brandy or milk, put into prepared cake tin - making a deep impression in the centre. Place in the middle of a moderate oven 150ºC, 350ºF or gas mark 2 for 2-2 ½ hours. Allow to cool in tin before turning out.

Cherry Cake

12 oz plain flour
8 oz margarine
2 oz ground almonds
4 eggs
2 level tsp baking powder

8 oz castor sugar
6 oz glace cherries
1 tsp almond essence (optional)
½ cup of milk

Cream margarine and sugar. Add egg yolks and beat well. Then add flour, milk, ground almonds and essence. Beat egg whites until stiff and fold into mixture. Add baking powder. Turn mixture into a greased and lined seven inch cake tin. Bake in the middle shelf at 160ºC, 320ºF or gas mark 3 for 1¼ hours.

Boiled Cake

8 oz plain flour
4 oz margarine
4 oz castor sugar
8 oz sultanas

1 egg
2 oz peel
1 level tsp baking soda
¼ pint milk

Boil margarine, sugar, fruit and milk for 10-15 minutes. Stir until it boils and then let simmer. Leave until cooled and put baking soda, flour and egg and mix well in saucepan. Bake for 1¼ hours. Start at moderate (200ºC) and check about an hour later and turn down to cool oven (150ºC).

Date & Walnut Loaf

8 oz self raising flour
1 packet of dates (chopped)
2 oz margarine
1 egg

1 level tsp baking soda
2 oz walnuts
2 oz sugar

Put chopped dates, sugar and margarine into a bowl and add ¼ pint of boiling water. Leave to cool, sieve flour and baking soda together and add to ingredients with egg and walnuts. Bake at 350ºF for 45 minutes.

Sherry Cake

4 oz self raising flour
4 oz Golden Fleece plain flour
12 oz sultanas
6 oz margarine
4 oz dark soft brown sugar
4 oz cherries, chopped

¼ pint sherry
2 large eggs, beaten lightly
1 level tbsp black treacle
1 level tsp baking soda
1 level tsp mixed spice

Grease and line the bottom of an eight inch round cake tin. Place sultanas into a sucepan with the sugar, margarine, treacle, baking soda, mixed spice and sherry. Stand over a low heat and stir occasionally until the ingredients have melted. Bring to the boil, reduce heat and simmer gently for 15 minutes stirring occasionally. Leave to cool. When cold stir in eggs, sifted flour and cherries to make a soft consistency. Turn mixture into tin and bake at 150ºC for about 2 hours or until a warmed skewer comes out clean. Remove from tin and cool. This cake will keep for up to six weeks if stored correctly.

Sponge Cake

4 large eggs
4 oz self raising flour

6 oz castor sugar
2 oz cornflour

Sift together flour and cornflour (twice). Beat together eggs and sugar until thick and creamy. Gradually fold in flour with a metal spoon. Divide between two seven and a half inch tins. Bake at gas mark 6 for about 20 minutes. Fill with seedless raspberry jam and fresh cream.

Fruit Cake

8 oz self raising flour
¼ tsp salt
4 oz margarine
4 oz castor sugar

a little grated orange peel
2 eggs
9 oz mixed fruit
⅛ pint milk

Cream margarine and sugar. Add eggs, sieve flour and fold into creamed mixture. Lastly add milk and fruit. Put into greased, lined loaf tin. Bake for 1¼ hours in a moderate oven 360ºF or until cooked. Make double the recipe and freeze one for again.

Victoria Sandwich Cake

4 eggs
8 oz self raising flour

8 oz soft margarine
8 oz castor sugar

Cream margarine and sugar until light and fluffy. Add eggs a little at a time. Fold in flour with a metal spoon. Divide mixture into two sandwich tins. Bake at 190ºC, gas mark 5 for 20-30 minutes. Sandwich together with butter cream icing.

Butter Sponge

8 oz self raising flour
8 oz castor sugar
4 tblsp hot water

8 oz margarine
4 eggs
vanilla, almond or coffee flavouring to taste

Cream margarine and sugar until light and fluffy. Add eggs one at a time beating well between each. Add flavouring then fold in flour quickly. Pour in down side of bowl the hot water and mix well in. Divide the mixture between two eight inch sandwich tins and bake in an oven heated at 400ºF and bake for 25 minutes. Fill with butter cream icing.

Orange Fruit Loaf

8 oz (225 g) self raising flour
4 oz (110 g) castor sugar
4 oz (110 g) margarine
3 oz (75 g) sultanas

1 oz (25g) cherries
5 tblsp of milk
1 beaten egg
rind and juice of one orange

Rub margarine into flour. Add rest of ingredients. Mix well together and turn into a lined loaf tin. Bake at 190ºC, 375ºF, gas mark 5 for 10 minutes then reduce heat to 180ºC, 350ºF, gas mark 4 for half to three quarters of an hour. Allow loaf to stand for at least one day before use.

Health Loaf

Put a beaker each of All-Bran, brown sugar, fruit or raisins in a bowl. Pour over a beaker of sweet milk. Leave for 20 minutes. Add a beaker of self raising flour, one teaspoon spice and one egg. Mix well and bake in a loaf tin for an hour in a moderate oven.

Quick Sweet Mince Ring

8 oz (225 g) self raising flour
6 oz (175 g) sweet mince
4 oz (110 g) castor sugar
2 oz (50 g) margarine

1 large egg
150 ml ($\frac{1}{4}$ pint) of milk to mix
$\frac{1}{2}$ tsp salt

Sieve flour and salt, rub in margarine, add sugar and sweet mince, mix together with beaten egg and milk. Turn into well greased metal ring mould. Place in centre of hot oven, 180°C, 350°F, gas mark 4 for 30-35 minutes. Turn out on to cooling tray and while still warm cover with thick vanilla icing, allowing it to trickle down the sides. Decorate with chopped nuts.

Carrot Cake

8 oz (225 g) self raising flour
2 tsp baking soda
5 oz (150 g) castor sugar
2 oz (50 g) walnuts, chopped
4 oz (100 g) carrots, peeled and grated

2 ripe bananas, mashed
2 eggs
$\frac{1}{4}$ pint (150 ml) sunflower oil
a little vanilla essence (optional)

TOPPING
3 oz (75 g) soft margarine
3 oz (75 g) cream cheese
6 oz (175 g) icing sugar, sieved

4 tblsp plain yoghurt
a little vanilla essence (optional)

Heat the oven to 350°F, gas 4 or 180°C. Grease and line an eight inch (20 cm) round cake tin with greased greaseproof paper. Measure the flour and baking powder into a large bowl and stir in the sugar. Add the nuts, carrots and bananas and mix lightly. Make a well in the centre, add the eggs and oil and beat well until blended, adding a little vanilla essence, if liked. Turn into the prepared tin and bake in the oven for 1¼ hours until the cake is golden brown and shrinking away from the sides of the tin. A warm skewer pushed into the centre should come out clean. Turn out, remove the paper, and leave to cool on a wire rack.

For the topping, measure all the ingredients into a bowl and beat well until bended and smooth. Spread over the cake and rough up with a fork. Leave in a cool place to harden slightly before serving. Serve, cut into thin wedges.

Victoria Sponge Cake *(makes 2 x 7 inch round)*

4 oz (100 g) castor sugar
4 oz (100 g) margarine
4 oz (100 g) plain flour

½ tsp baking powder
2 eggs, lightly beaten

Pre-heat oven to 240ºC, 475ºF, gas mark 9. Prepare baking tins. Lightly grease then dust with flour. Shake off excess flour. Cream together sugar and margarine until light and fluffy. Gradually add beaten eggs. Sieve together flour and baking powder and lightly fold into mixture. Divide mixture into prepared tins and bake for approximately 12-15 minutes. When baked turn out on to a wire rack to cool. When completely cool sandwich together with jam and vanilla buttercream.

Gingerbread

8 oz plain flour
pinch of salt
3 tsp ground ginger
4 oz butter or margarine
1 tsp bicarbonate of soda

1½ oz soft brown sugar
4 oz golden syrup
4 oz black treacle
1 egg, beaten
½ pint warm milk

Sieve flour, salt and ginger in a bowl. Gently heat the butter, brown sugar, syrup and treacle in a saucepan until the fat melts. Sprinkle the bicarbonate of soda into the warmed milk. Gradually beat the melted butter and treacle mixture into the dry ingredients until smooth. Finally beat in the egg and milk. Pour into prepared seven inch square cake tin greased and lined. Cook for 1¼ hours in a moderate oven. Cool slightly in the tin before turning out on a wire rack. Store in foil or an airtight tin. Serve in slices plain or buttered. Oven 170ºC, 350ºF or gas mark 4.

Easy Made Chocolate Cake

4 oz self raising flour
2 oz drinking chocolate
1 tsp baking powder
3 eggs

5 oz castor sugar
2 dsp spoonfuls of milk
3 oz margarine

Place all ingredients into food mixer together and mix at fast speed for five minutes. Put into two seven inch sandwich tins and bake at 350ºF, 180ºC or gas mark 4. When cooled fill with butter chocolate cream.

Boiled Cake

½ lb margarine
1 cup sultanas
1 cup sugar
1 ½ cups water
1 cup raisins

1 cup currants
3 cups plain flour
1 tsp baking soda
½ tsp mixed spice

Put raisins, sultanas, currants, sugar, margarine and water into a saucepan and bring to the boil. Cool well and add baking soda, flour, spice and eggs. Put into lined tin and bake for about 1½ hours in a moderate oven.

Chestnut Meringue Gateau

6 oz minced walnuts (put in a cool oven to dry off)
12 oz castor sugar
rum or vanilla flavouring
few walnut halves

6 egg whites
1 tin chestnut puree
½ pint cream

Make meringue mixture from egg whites and sugar. Fold in walnuts. Form into two rounds on lined baking trays. Bake for one hour in a slow oven. Cool and fill with whipped cream and chestnut puree combined and flavoured with rum or vanilla, reserving some for the top as well. Decorate with walnut halves.

Chocolate Cake

5 oz plain flour
1½ oz drinking chocolate
6 oz castor sugar
6 oz margarine

4 dsp milk
3 eggs
3 level tsp baking powder

Put all the ingredients into a mixing bowl except the baking powder and beat until smooth, then add baking powder and beat for a few minutes. Put into a six or seven inch sandwich tin for 10 minutes at gas mark 6 or 400ºF. Then reduce heat to gas mark 4 or 350ºF for 30 minutes. When cool sandwich together with butter cream.

Coffee Cream Gateau

SPONGE:

2 oz butter
4 oz castor sugar
pinch of salt
4 eggs
5 oz plain flour
2-3 drops vanilla essence

FILLING:

8 oz butter
1 tbsp cocoa powder, sieve together
1-2 tblsp coffee liqueur
4 oz icing sugar
1 tblsp coffee essence

Melt butter and allow to cool. To make sponge - whisk eggs and sugar together in a bowl until thick and creamy. Sieve flour and salt together. Fold through egg mixture using a metal spoon. Lastly stir in cooled melted butter and vanilla essence. Pour into a prepared eight inch tin buttered and dusted with flour. Bake at 180ºC, 350ºF for 35-45 minutes until well risen and set. Cool on a wire tray.

Cream together softened butter, icing sugar and cocoa, until smooth and well blended. Stir in coffee essence and coffee liqueur to taste.

Divide cooled sponge in three. Spread coffee cream on each layer and sandwich together using a palette knife dipped in hot water. Smooth coffee cream over top and sides of sponge. Pipe remaining filling on top, decorate with walnuts.

Chocolate Cake

5 oz plain flour
1½ oz drinking chocolate
6 oz castor sugar
6 oz margarine

4 dsp milk
3 eggs
3 level tsp baking powder

Put all ingredients into a bowl except the baking powder. Beat until smooth then add baking powder and beat again. Divide mixture into two six inch sandwich tins and bake in an oven at 380ºF for 10 minutes then 355ºF for 15-20 minutes.

Treacle Gingerbread

8 oz butter
8 oz treacle
8 oz brown sugar
12 oz plain flour
2 level tsp ginger

2 level tsp cinnamon
2 level tsp baking soda
½ pint milk
2 large eggs, beaten

Melt butter, sugar and treacle in a pan. Sift flour, ginger and cinnamon. Stir into melted mixture with beaten egg. Warm milk to blood heat and pour on to baking soda, mix all the ingredients. Pour into loaf tin. Bake at gas mark 2 for 1½ hours. Cover with tin foil after one hour.

Lemon Cheesecake with Kiwi *(serves 8)*

1 12 inch flan case (sponge)
FILLING
11 oz (2 x 150 g) tubs of natural yoghurt
3 tbsp castor sugar
juice and grated rind of half a lemon
2 fl oz white grape juice or apple juice

½ oz (15 g) gelatine
8 fl oz (250 ml) ½ pint double cream
TOPPING
3 kiwis sliced to decorate top
Reserve a little whipped cream to decorate top with rossettes

Mix together yoghurt, sugar, lemon rind and juice of lemon in a bowl. Pour juice of grape or apple into a separate bowl. Set over simmering water and sprinkle over gelatine. Stir until gelatine has melted, cool slightly, then quickly stir in the yoghurt mixture. Whisk cream to soft peaks and fold into yoghurt mixture. Pour into flan case, chill for one hour and cover with kiwi slices and cream.

Pineapple Cake with a Difference

4 oz butter or margarine
6 oz granulated sugar
12 oz self raising flour
1 tsp mixed spice
12 oz mixed fruit

1 tsp bicarbonate of soda
2 eggs
12 oz crushed pineapple

Put sugar, butter, fruit, pineapple with juice, spice and bicarbonate of soda into a saucepan and slowly bring to the boil. Boil for three minutes and allow to cool completely. Add the flour and two well beaten eggs and mix well. Place the mix into a tin (greased and lined with greaseproof paper) and bake for 90 minutes at 300ºC. If you can't wait to sample your masterpiece top a warm slice with fresh cream.

Lemon Gateau

6 oz margarine or butter
6 oz castor sugar
1tsp finely grated lemon zest
3 large eggs

1 tsp lemon juice
6 oz self raising flour or plain flour
1 ½ tsp baking powder

Cream fat and sugar until soft and light. Gradually beat in eggs. Sieve flour and baking powder into mixture. Add lemon juice. Put into two greased seven or eight inch tins. Bake for about 18 minutes at 350ºF or 180ºC. Blend ½ lb lemon curd with ¼ pint whipped cream for filling and top. Decorate with lemon slices.

Small Cakes, Biscuits & Tray Bakes

Viennese Shortbread

4 oz margarine
1 oz icing sugar
4 oz plain flour

4 drops vanilla essence
1 small packet Scotchbloc chocolate

You will need one large icing bag and one rosette nozzle and greased swiss roll tins or a large tray.
Put margarine into food mixer bowl. Sieve in the icing sugar and beat until creamy, add vanilla essence and beat. Then add flour until mixture resembles a thick paste, only mix till flour is totally incorporated. Chill mixture, then fill a piping bag with a rosette nozzle. Pipe rosettes on to the tray, medium size. Bake in an oven 180-190ºC or 350-375ºF for approximately 10-15 minutes. Cool on a tray. Melt chocolate and put a teaspoonful on each biscuit. To make 3 ½ dozen approximately multiply basic recipe by 4.

Almond Cheese Cakes

3 oz ground almonds
1 oz melted butter or margarine for binding
shortcrust pastry

2 oz castor sugar
1 egg
1 egg yolk

Bind dry ingredients. Divide into patty tins lined with pastry. Bake for 15-20 minutes in a moderate oven gas mark 6 or 425ºF.

Date & Almond Slice

150 g white Scotchbloc
1 egg, separated
100 g dried dates, chopped
50 g ground almonds

50 g self raising flour
30 ml milk
5 ml baking powder
almond essence

Base line and grease a seven inch round cake tin. Melt the Scotchbloc, cool slightly then whisk in the egg yolk. Add the dates, almonds, flour, milk, baking powder and a few drops of almond essence. Mix well and carefully fold in stiffly beaten egg white. Spoon the mixture into the tin and level. Bake at 180ºC, 350ºF or gas mark 4 for about 25 minutes or until golden. Turn out. Serve warm or cold, cut into fingers.

Sugar Pastry

8 oz (200 g) plain flour
pinch of salt
1 egg

2 oz (50 g) castor sugar
5 oz (125 g) butter or margarine

Lightly beat together the egg and sugar. Add the butter or margarine and mix lightly. Gradually add the flour and salt. Mix lightly until smooth. Chill before using.

All Butter Shortbread *(makes 12 biscuits)*

4 oz (100 g) butter
6 oz (150 g) plain flour

2 oz (50 g) castor sugar
pinch of salt

Sieve together flour and salt. Cream together butter and sugar until light and fluffy. Add flour and mix to a smooth firm dough. Chill for one hour then roll on a lightly floured board to approximately ½cm (¾ inch) thick. Cut into rounds using a fluted pastry cutter. Place on a baking sheet and bake for approximately 15-20 minutes at 240ºC, 475ºF, gas mark 9. When baked allow to cool slightly then dust with castor sugar.

Shortcrust Pastry

8 oz (200 g) plain flour
pinch of salt
2-3 tbsp water

2 oz (50 g) lard
2 oz (50 g) margarine

Sieve together flour and salt. Rub in lard and margarine until mixture resembles fine breadcrumbs. Make a well in the centre. Add sufficient chilled water to form a firm paste. Chill before using.

Coconut Cakes

PASTRY:
8 oz plain flour
4 oz margarine
1/2 oz castor sugar
egg yolk

FILLING:
2 egg whites
1 tbsp cold water
4 oz castor sugar
4 oz coconut

Rub margarine into flour. Mix sugar and egg together. Mix well with flour to make a stiff dough. Roll out and line bun tin and put a little jam in each. Beat egg whites until stiff, add water and beat in half of the sugar. Fold in the other half and coconut then mix well. Divide into pastry tins. Bake in a moderate 350ºF oven until pale in colour.

Apple Flan

1 x 12 inch sponge flan bought or home baked
1 lb cooking apples, peeled, chopped and stewed
½ pint fresh whipping cream

1 flake bar
little apple jelly or marmalade to coat base of flan case

Put flan case on serving dish, coat base thinly with apple jelly or marmalade. Add stewed apples, cover with firmly beaten whipped cream. Sprinkle with flake bar crumbled over cream and serve. Serves 8 portions.

Nutty Truffles

8 oz icing sugar
4 oz margarine (add 2 tblsp of cocoa to this and sugar)
2 oz cherries, chopped
2 tbsp hazelnut chocolate spread

1 oz toasted coconut (browned under grill)
2 oz walnuts chopped (hazelnuts can be used)
1 large packet Scotchbloc chocolate

Make buttercream with icing sugar and margarine. Add the cocoa powder beat in, then add all the other ingredients except the chocolate. Make into small balls, leave to harden. Coat with melted chocolate, place on greaseproof paper. Can be put into the freezer when set. When lifted out of the freezer allow truffles to sit until moisture has dried from the chocolate. (Beware of little mice.) Do this in a safe place. These truffles can be made from left over buttercream and remaining ingredients from a large baking. These quantities are only a guide.

Caramel Slices

SHORTBREAD:
4 oz margarine
2 oz castor sugar
1 oz cornflour
1 oz farola
4 oz flour

CARAMEL:
4 oz margarine
3 oz sugar
1 dsp syrup
1 tin Ideal milk

Cream margarine and sugar, add flour, farola and cornflour. Place on a baking sheet. Put caramel ingredients into saucepan and boil for 20 minutes. Spread caramel on shortbread and cover with melted chocolate. When cool cut into squares.

Crunchies

8 oz plain flour
4 oz oatflakes
5 oz margarine
3 oz brown sugar

FILLING:
2 oz margarine
8 oz mixed fruit
vanilla essence
3 oz sugar
1 egg

Melt margarine and sugar, take off the heat and stir in mixed flour and oatflakes. Press half the mixture into greased swiss roll tin. Spread the filling over the base and cover with remainder of mixture. Bake in oven for 20-30 minutes until brown. Cut into squares while hot. TO MAKE FILLING: Melt margarine and sugar over a low heat. Add fruit and cook slightly. Allow to cool then add the beaten egg and essence. Stir well.

Flakemeal Biscuits

4 oz wheatmeal
4 oz sugar
1 pinch baking powder

8 oz flaked meal
8 oz butter or margarine

Cream butter or margarine with sugar. Add other ingredients. Roll out and cut into rounds. Cook in a slow oven about 300ºF.

Shortbread

8 oz butter
 4 oz cornflour
pinch of salt

4 oz castor sugar
8 oz plain flour

Cream the butter and sugar until white and fluffy. Sieve the dry ingredients and add to the creamed mixture. Knead until smooth. Press into a twelve by eight inch tin. Smooth over the top. Mark into fingers. Prick with a fork. Bake in a slow oven 325ºF or gas mark 3 for 30-40 minutes. Re-cut the fingers and dredge with castor sugar while still hot. Leave until cold, remove from the tin.

Melting Moments

7 oz margarine
3 oz icing sugar
1 tsp vanilla essence

4 oz cornflour
4 oz plain flour

Cream margarine and sugar, add cornflour, plain flour and essence. Make into small balls and place on a baking tray. Cook very slowly until golden brown at gas mark 3. When cool join together with butter icing.

Adelaide Cakes *(makes 12-14 cakes)*

4 oz butter
2 oz cherries, chopped
3 eggs
2 oz cornflour
1 tbsp milk (if necessary)

4 oz castor sugar
1 oz almond, chopped
4 oz flour
2 level tsp baking powder

Cream butter and sugar. Mix in cherries and almonds. Add eggs one at a time and beat well Mix flour and baking powder into creamed mixture. Add milk, if necessary, to make a fairly soft mixture. Bake until golden brown and firm to the touch in an oven at 350ºF, gas mark 4 for 15-20 minutes.

Marshmallow Fingers

BASE:
10 oz margarine
4 oz castor sugar
1 lb flour
pinch of salt
pinch of baking powder

TOPPING:
1 jelly
4 oz icing sugar
½ pint cold water
coconut

Cream margarine and sugar. Add flour and mix well. Turn into a lightly greased swiss roll tin. Cook in a moderate oven 375ºF until golden brown. When base is cool spread on the topping. TOPPING: Steep jelly in ½ pint cold water for 10 minutes. Boil exactly 8 minutes. Add 4 oz icing sugar when jelly is cool beat until stiff. Spread on the base and sprinkle with coconut. When set cut into fingers.

Coconut Tartlets

PASTRY:
8 oz plain flour
1 egg approximately
6 oz soft margarine
2 oz castor sugar

TOPPING:
4 oz dessicated coconut
1-2 small eggs to bind coconut and sugar
4 oz castor sugar

FILLING: 1 Jar raspberry Jam

Make as for shortcrust pastry. Roll out ¼ inch thick. Cut into rounds with a four inch fluted cutter. Line patty tins. Put ¼ spoonful of raspberry jam in each case and cover with dsp of coconut mixture. Bake in an oven 350ºF, 180ºC - 375ºF, 190ºC for 30 minutes until pastry base is golden and coconut top is golden. Cool and serve. Freezes well.

Coburg Cakes *(makes 16 cakes)*

2 oz butter
1 egg
1½ level tsp cinnamon
1 level tsp treacle
milk

2½ oz castor sugar
5 oz flour
1 level tsp bicarbonate of soda
1 level tsp syrup
almond split

Cream butter and sugar, add beaten egg and flour alternatively. Mix in the rest of the ingredients. Beat in treacle and syrup, add milk to make a dropping consistency. Put half almond at the bottom of each baking case. Three quarters fill baking cases. Bake in a moderate oven at 400ºF middle shelf for 15 minutes.

Almond Slices

PASTRY:
8 oz plain flour
1 egg approximately

FILLING:
1 Jar raspberry Jam

TOPPING:
3 oz self raising flour

3 oz castor sugar
1 large egg
a little milk if required

ICING:
6 oz seived icing sugar
2 oz coconut - toasted under the grill or
2 oz chopped walnuts or almonds
a little water to make icing spreadable but not runny

Make pastry as for shortcrust pastry, line a swiss roll tin thinly. Coat well with raspberry jam. Put flour, margarine, castor sugar, egg and almond essence into food mixer bowl. Beat for 2 minutes, cover with jam. Put into oven 350ºF, 180ºC or 375ºF, 190ºC for 40 minutes until top is spongy and when pressed by a finger bounces back. Cool and ice with water icing and sprinkle coconut or nuts on while still soft. When icing has set, cut into slices.

Coconut Buns

6 oz plain flour
2 eggs
4-6 chopped cherries
5 oz castor sugar

3 oz margarine
6 oz coconut
cold water

Sieve the flour and rub in the margarine. Add the water and bind. Roll out and cut, placing in patty tins. Beat the eggs and mix in the coconut, castor sugar and chopped cherries. Put a blob of jam in each pastry case and top with the egg mixture. Bake for 20-25 minutes at 300ºF, 150ºC, gas mark 3.

Almond Bakewell Buns

6 oz plain flour
4 oz margarine
4 oz castor sugar
½ tsp almond essence
2 tblsp apricot jam

3 oz margarine
cold water
4 oz ground rice or semolina
1 egg, beaten
few flaked almonds

Sieve the flour and rub in the margarine. Add the water and bind. Roll out and cut, placing in patty tins. Melt margarine in pan, add sugar, ground rice, almond essence and egg. Put a blob of jam in each pastry case and top with the mixture. Sprinkle with almond flakes. Bake for 20-25 minutes at 350ºF, 180ºC, gas mark 4.

Gravy Rings

6 oz plain flour
1 egg
2 oz margarine
1 oz castor sugar

castor sugar and cinnamon to coat
1 tsp baking powder
a little milk

Sieve flour and baking powder. Rub in margarine, add sugar, mix with egg and add a little milk if necessary. Roll out and cut out with circular cutter. Fry in deep fat for 6 minutes. Toss in castor sugar with cinnamon added.

Mars Bars

8 oz flour
3 oz castor sugar
3 oz margarine

FILLING:
1 tblsp syrup
4 oz margarine
1 tin condensed milk
4 oz sugar

Cream margarine, sugar and flour together. Press into a swiss roll tin and bake until brown at gas mark 5. Boil ingredients for filling for about 15 minutes or until it thickens slightly and gets a little darker. Pour on top of base. Top with ½ bar melted chocolate

Viennese Whirls

1 lb plain flour
6 oz icing sugar

1 lb margarine
1 tsp vanilla essence

Cream margarine until creamy white. Add in vanilla essence. Beat in flour slowly. Pipe out on to a floured baking tray. Bake at gas mark 4-5 for 10-15 minutes.

Snowballs

8 oz digestive biscuits
1½ dsp drinking chocolate
small tin of condensed milk

2 oz margarine
marshmallows
coconut

Melt margarine in a saucepan, add crushed biscuits, chocolate powder and milk and mix well. Keep hands damp and place a small amount of mixture in palm and flatten, place marshmallow in centre and cover with the mixture. Shape into balls and roll in coconut.

Peppermint Slices

BISCUIT BASE:
1 1/2 cups self raising flour
1 1/2 cups brown sugar
1 cup coconut
6 oz butter

ICING:
12 oz icing sugar
3 tblsp milk
1 block chocolate
2 oz lard
1 tblsp peppermint essence

Mix all dry ingredients for biscuit base together, add melted butter. Mix well. Press into greased swiss roll tin and bake in a moderate oven for 20 minutes. While still warm top with icing. Sift sugar, add melted lard, milk and essence and mix well. Spread over biscuit and when cold top with melted chocolate.

Walnut & Coconut Fingers

6 oz short pastry
apricot jam
4 oz icing sugar
2 oz chopped walnuts
white of 1 egg

ALTERNATIVE FILLING:
2 oz castor sugar
white of 1 egg
2 oz dessiccated coconut.

Line a swiss roll tin with shortcake pastry. Spread thickly with jam. Slightly beat white of egg. Add other ingredients and spread over jam. Bake at 325ºF, gas mark 3 for about 15 minutes until golden brown. Cut into fingers while still hot. Leave to cool in tin.

Fruit Squares

4 oz raisins (or mixed fruit)
4 oz sultanas (or mixed fruit)
4 oz sugar
1 good tblsp flour

½ tsp spice
1 grated cooking apple (optional)
2 tblsp mince meat (optional)
1 large cup of water

Put all ingredients into a saucepan and bring to the boil. Simmer for 5 minutes until tender. Cool before use. Make short pastry about 12 oz, roll out and bake in swiss roll tin.

Poor Man's Florentines

8 oz digestive biscuits
4 g margarine
1 oz brown sugar

TOPPING:
4 g chopped cherries
4 g chopped walnuts
2 g flaked almonds
1 small tin condensed milk

Melt margarine. Add crushed biscuits and sugar and put into a swiss roll tin. TOPPING: Spread chopped ingredients over biscuit mixture. Trickle one small tin of sweetened condensed milk over the top. Bake for 20 minutes at 350ºF, 180ºC. Cut into squares when cold.

Shortbread

½ lb butter
8 oz plain flour

4 oz icing sugar
4 oz cornflour

Cream butter and icing sugar until creamy. Add sieved flour and cornflour. Roll out and cut into rounds. Bake at 325ºF until light golden brown for 20-30 minutes.

Coconut Munchies

1/2 bar chocolate
1 egg
4 oz castor sugar

4 oz fine coconut
4 oz cherries

Line swiss roll tin with grease proof paper. Melt chocolate and pour into tin. Leave to set. Beat egg and castor sugar together until stiff, add coconut and cherries. Place on top of chocolate and bake at 350ºF, gas mark 4 for about 20 minutes. When cool cut into fingers.

Shortbread

8 oz butter
9 oz plain flour

4 oz castor sugar
3 oz cornflour

Melt butter in a saucepan and add all other ingredients. Do not over heat butter. Spread in a swiss roll tin. Cook in a moderate oven.

Apricot Nutty Fingers

6 oz shortcrust pastry	4 oz sugar
2 oz coconut	2 oz dates, chopped
2 oz walnuts	2 oz cherries
1 beaten egg	apricot jam

Melt margarine in a saucepan, add crushed biscuits, chocolate powder and milk and mix well. Keep hands damp and place a small amount of mixture in palm and flatten, place marshmallow in centre and cover with the mixture. Shape into balls and roll in coconut.

Fudge Squares

4 oz castor sugar	7½ oz digestive biscuits, crushed
4 oz margarine	1 oz walnuts
1 oz cherries	2 small tblsp syrup
small tin of condensed milk	handful of sultanas
10 square Scotchbloc chocolate	

Put castor sugar, margarine, syrup and condensed milk into a saucepan and cook for 5 minutes. Add crushed biscuits, chopped walnuts and cherries and sultanas. Spread on a baking tray and leave in fridge to set. Cover with ten squares of Scotchbloc.

Shortbread

8 oz butter	10 oz plain flour
4 oz sugar	2 oz cornflour

Cream butter and sugar then add flour and cornflour. Knead well and cut into shapes. Bake in a moderate oven depending on thickness.

Jumble Biscuits

4 oz butter	4 oz castor sugar
10 oz flour	2 level tsp baking powder
1 egg	

Cream butter and sugar. Mix flour and baking powder. Add beaten egg and flour. Mix well into creamed mixture. Knead, roll out a quarter inch thick. Cut into biscuit shapes. Put on to greased baking sheet. Bake for 10 minutes in an oven at 350ºF.

Peanut Cookies

4 oz margarine
1 tblsp syrup
4 oz porridge oats
2 oz salted peanuts

4 oz granulated sugar
4 oz self-raising flour
¼ tsb bicarbonate of soda

Melt margarine, sugar and syrup in a saucepan. Remove from heat and stir in flour, porridge oats and peanuts. Beat well and roll into walnut size balls and place well apart on a greased baking tray. Cook at 350ºF, 180ºC, gas mark 4 for 15 minutes. Cool for 5 minutes before lifting on to a wire rack.

Shortbread

8 oz butter
4 oz icing sugar

4 oz cornflour
8 oz self raising flour

Cream butter and sugar and then add flour and cornflour. Cut into shapes and bake at 3500F for 25 minutes.

Custard Creams

7 oz packet of Marie Biscuits
10 oz walnuts
1 egg
2 ½ oz coconut

4 oz margarine
1 ½ oz sugar
1 tsp cocoa

BASE: Melt margarine, sugar and cocoa in a pan. Add beaten egg and remove from heat. Mix with broken biscuits, chopped walnuts and coconut. Spread in swiss roll tin.
FILLING: Cream 5 oz icing sugar, 2 oz butter, 1 tblsp custard powder, 1 tbls hot water. Spread over biscuit base.
TOPPING: Melt 4 oz chocolate and 2 oz margarine together and spread over creamed mixture. When cooled, cut into fingers.

Flakemeal Biscuits

4 oz margarine
4 oz flakemeal
3 oz plain flour
pinch of baking powder

2 oz coconut
2 oz sugar
pinch of salt

Cream margarine and sugar, then add flour and cut into shapes. Put on a baking tray which has been lightly sprinkled with flour. Cook at 200ºC until golden brown.

Flakemeal Biscuits

6 oz plain flour
1/4 tsp baking soda (dissolved in 2 tsp hot water)
8 oz flakemeal

6 oz margarine
4 oz castor sugar

Cream margarine and sugar. Put in baking soda, gradually add flour and flakemeal. Roll out and cut into biscuits. Bake for 20 minutes at 350ºF, dust with castor sugar.

Toffee Shortbread

BASE:
10 oz flour
6 oz sugar
8 oz margarine

TOFFEE:
6 oz margarine
5 oz castor sugar
4 tblsp syrup
1 small tin Nestles condensed milk

BASE: Make shortbread and put in greased swiss roll tin and bake.
Melt margarine, add ingredients. Stir with wooden spoon and boil for 5 minutes. Pour quickly on shortbread base and cool. Cover with melted chocolate. Cool and cut into fingers.

Flakemeal Shortbread

8 oz margarine
1 level tsp salt
4 oz castor sugar
pinch baking powder

10 oz flakemeal
2 tblsp ground almonds
4 oz plain flour

Cream margarine and sugar together. Gradually work in other ingredients. Turn on to a floured board. Sprinkle with flakemeal and roll out. Score with a fork to roughen. Cut into biscuits and bake on a greased baking sheet at 350ºF until light golden brown.

Caramel Squares

BASE:
5 oz plain flour
2 oz castor sugar
4 oz butter or margarine
CARAMEL:
4 oz sugar

4 oz butter or margarine
few drops of vanilla essence
2 tblsp syrup
small tin condensed milk
TOPPING:
½ block cooking chocolate

Sieve flour and rub in margarine. Add sugar. Press into greased swiss roll tin. Bake in oven at 350ºF, 175ºC or gas mark 4. Put sugar, syrup, margarine and condensed milk into a saucepan. When sugar is dissolved bring to the boil and cook gently for 5 minutes, stirring occasionally. Add vanilla essence. Pour on to cooked base and leave to set and cool. Cover with melted chocolate. When set cut into squares.

Almond Fingers

PASTRY:
5 oz flour
1 egg yolk and a little water to mix
3 oz margarine
pinch of salt
raspberry jam

FILLING:
6 oz castor sugar
2 egg whites
1 oz flaked almonds
3 oz ground almonds
a few drops of almond essence

Sieve flour and salt. Cut and rub in margarine, mix to stiff dough with egg yolk and water. Turn unto a floured board and roll to fit a swiss roll tin. Spread lightly with jam.
FILLING: Whisk the white of eggs a little - not necessary to have them really stiff. Fold in sugar, ground almonds and almond essence. Spread over jam and sprinkle with shredded almonds. Bake in a moderate oven for 40 minutes then cut into fingers. Leave in tin until cold.

Non Bakes

Lemon Coconut Squares

8 oz Marie biscuits
4 oz margarine
4 dsp lemon juice

4 oz coconut
1 tin condensed milk

Melt margarine, milk and lemon juice in a saucepan, add crushed biscuits and coconut. Spread in a swiss roll tin. Cover with icing and sprinke with coconut. When set cut into squares.

Mars Crunchies

3 Mars Bars
3 oz butter or margarine

3 cups Rice Krispies
cherries or walnuts (if liked)

Melt margarine and Mars Bars in a saucepan slowly. Transfer hot liquid to bowl containing Rice Krispies and cherries or walnuts which have been chopped. Mix all together and press into a tray or square sandwich tin to set. Then cut into fingers or squares.

Fifteens

15 digestive biscuits
15 chopped cherries

15 pink/white marshmallows chopped
1 small tin Nestles sweetened condensed milk

Mix all ingredients together and form into a long roll. Sprinkle a little coconut on a piece of greaseproof paper, place roll on the paper and shape to approximately 1½ inches in diameter. Leave rolled in paper in the fridge to firm up. Then cut into slices.

Peanut Squares

1 jar crunchy peanut butter
1 large packet Rich Tea biscuits, crushed

4 oz margarine
6 tblsp of syrup

Melt margarine, sugar, syrup and peanut butter in a saucepan. Add crushed biscuits and mix well. Put into a swiss roll tin. Leave to cool. Cover with melted chocolate. Cut into squares.

Coconut Balls

2 oz butter
3 oz coconut
1 cup cornflakes

1/2 cup sugar
6 oz margarine

Melt the margarine in a pan and add the dry ingredients mixing well. Bake in a greased swiss roll tin in a moderate oven 350ºF, 180ºC, gas mark 4. Allow to cool. Melt ½ a block of cooking chocolate and spread over the cooled biscuits. When set, cut into squares.

Coconut Bake

1 cup flour	1 cup cornflakes
1 cup coconut	½ cup sugar
2 tblsp drinking chocolate	6 oz margarine

Melt the margarine in a pan and add the dry ingredients mixing well. Bake in a greased swiss roll tin in a moderate oven 350ºF, 180ºC, gas mark 4. Allow to cool. Melt ½ a block of cooking chocolate and spread over the cooled biscuits. When set, cut into squares.

Chocolate Fancies

8 oz margarine	8 oz castor sugar
2 beaten eggs	4-6 chopped cherries
8 oz Rich Tea biscuits, crushed	3 dsp drinking chocolate

Melt margarine and sugar, add eggs and boil for 5 minutes. Add drinking chocolate and crushed biscuits. Add cherries. Put into a swiss roll tin and allow to cool. Melt ½ block of cooking chocolate and spread over the cooled base. When set, cut into squares.

Raspberry Ruffle Bars

8 oz coconut	1 packet raspberry jelly crystals
1 small tin condensed milk	

Mix coconut and raspberry jelly together. Add tin of condensed milk. Press into a swiss roll tin. Cover with 1/2 block of melted cooking chocolate. When set cut into squares.

Coffee Roll

8 oz packet of digestive biscuits	cooking chocolate
butter icing	1 small tin sweetened condensed milk
4 oz icing sugar	3 tblsp ground almonds

Crush biscuits and mix all dry ingredients together. Add milk and coffee. Roll out on a board sprinkled with icing sugar - about 12 x 6 inches. Spread with butter icing and roll up like a swiss roll. Cover with melted chocolate. Slice when cold.

Mars Crunchies

FUDGE FILLING:	2 dsp syrup
4 oz margarine	1 small tin condensed milk
2 oz castor sugar	8 oz cooking chocolate
	small packet of cracker bread

Line a swiss roll tin with greaseproof paper. Spread 4 oz melted chocolate in tin. Place cracker bread on top of chocolate. FILLING: Melt margarine, sugar and syrup. Add condensed milk and stir continuously until it thickens and is a golden colour. Spread on top of cracker bread. Add another layer of cracker bread and cover with 4 oz melted chocolate. Cut into fingers.

Starters

Prawn Cocktail *(Serves 4)*

4 oz prawns	4 drops of tobasco
2 tblsp tomato ketchup	1 tblsp sweet sherry
3 tblsp mayonnaise	2 tsp fresh cream

Stir all ingredients into a bowl and place in the fridge for at least an hour before serving. Serve in a tall glass on a bed of shredded lettuce with a slice of lemon on the rim and the prawns and sauce sprinkled with a little cayenne pepper.

Minted Melon

2 small melons	4 oz seedless green grapes
2 tblsp Colman's sweet mint jelly	2 kiwi fruit, peeled and sliced
1 large pear or green apple (quartered and sliced)	1 small banana, sliced

Cut melons in half in a zig-zag pattern. Discard seeds. Remove melon flesh with melon baller. Place melon balls and grapes into a glass bowl with mint jelly and chilll overnight. Add remaining fruit about one hour before serving. Serve inside melon shells.

Chicken Broth

1 chicken carcass and any left-over chicken	1 tsp salt
6 peppercorns finely crushed	1 bay leaf
1 bouquet garni	2 carrots, peeled and sliced
3 celery sticks	2 oz barley or soup mixture

Put carcass and any chicken pieces into a large pan, cover with cold water and add rest of ingredients. Bring to the boil, lower heat and gently simmer for 2 hours. Skin off scum at intervals with a slotted spoon. Add a little more water if liquid in pan begins to get low. Remove carcass before serving, also bay leaf and bouquet garni. Adjust seasoning if necessary and serve sprinkled with chopped parsley.

Tomato Soup

1 small onion	salt and pepper
1 stick celery	1 oz ham, ham bone or bacon rinds
1 oz butter or margarine	1 bouquet garni
1 pint tomato pulp or 1 lb fresh tomatoes	1 pint stock or water
1½ oz flour	½ pint milk

Chop onion, carrot, celery and ham and sweat in the melted butter for 15 minutes. Add seasoning, bouquet garni, tomato pulp and stock. Simmer together for an hour to an hour and a half. Sieve then re-heat and thicken with the blended flour and milk. The addition of a little cream is an improvement to this soup. But add it just before serving.

Winter Soup

8 oz potatoes
8 oz carrots
8 oz onions
8 oz turnip
1 parsnip

1 oz butter
1½ pints water
½ pint milk
seasoning
chopped parsley

Clean and prepare the vegetables. Cut into small pieces. Melt the butter in a large saucepan and cook vegetables for a few minutes. Add about 1¼ pints of water and a little seasoning. Bring this to the boil and simmer until the vegetables are tender. Mix in flour with a little water to a smooth paste and add vegetables. Put mixture through a sieve, return to saucepan. Add milk and seasoning. Bring to the boil. Just before serving sprinkle with a little chopped parsley.

Savoury Melon With Ham

8 lettuce leaves
5 fl oz natural yoghurt
2 tsp horseradish sauce

1 tsp mustard
4 slices lean ham
1 small melon, peeled, seeded and cut into thin strips

Arrange the lettuce leaves on four small serving plates. In a small mixing bowl, mix together the yoghurt, horseradish and mustard. Spread over one side of each ham slice and roll up. Arrange the ham and melon on the lettuce.

Mushroom Soup

2 oz butter
2 spring onions, finely chopped
8 oz mushrooms, sliced
10 fl oz chicken stock

10 fl oz milk
1 tbsp flour
salt and pepper
5 fl oz single cream

Melt three quarters of the butter in a saucepan. Add the spring onions and mushrooms and fry for 3 minutes. Pour in the stock and milk, bring to the boil and simmer, covered for 20 minutes. Rub though a strainer or puree in an electric blender. Melt the remaining butter in the rinsed-out pan. Stir in the pureed soup and bring to the boil. Season to taste and stir in the cream. Serve.

Ulster Salad

Baby Gems
Mushrooms
Smoked bacon lardons
Soda bread

Black pudding (specific brand)
Tomato based chutney
Poached egg

At the same time fry off bacon lardons, sliced mushrooms, black pudding in the pan. Meanwhile dice up soda bread and either deep fry or coat in olive oil and bake in the oven at 200 deg until golden and crisp. Add tomato relish to the pan. Bring a pot of water to the boil for poaching an egg, preferable temperature 93ºC. Bring pot to the boil then turn down heat. Add tsp of white vinegar to the hot water. Whisk the water and when it is at a gentle swirling motion add egg to the centre of the pan. Let the egg settle . Toss baby gems lightly in a dressing of your choice, preferably olive oil or honey and mustard. Add croutons and hot ingredients to the salad, gently toss, serve in a salad bowl and place poached egg on top. (Croutons can be precooked and ready to use)

Smoked Salmon & Buttermilk Pancakes on Cashel Blue Crème Fraiche

1 pt buttermilk
200 g self raising flour
Salt and pepper

Butter for the pan
100 g crème fraiche
Cashel blue cheese

Sieve flour into bowl. Add buttermilk. Whisk until smooth shiny consistency until batter holds a figure of 8. Preheat a four inch pan with a knob of butter. Add fine slices of smoked salmon then add a ladel full of batter until the salmon is covered and the pan is three quarters full. Reduce heat of pan and, once with a pallet knife, carefully loosen the pancake from the rim of the pan. Optional – to seal the top of the pancake to make it easier to turn, place under grill until the top is set. After doing this the pancake should turn over with no difficulty. Return to cooker on a low heat and cook until the pancake has risen and adapted a golden brown colour. Dressing – this is best made before pancakes and left to mature. Place crème fraiche and Cashel blue cheese into a food processer (chopped parsley is optional) along with some milk or cream and blend the dressing until it is of the constituency of coating the back of a spoon. Serve – On a bed of watercress place a pancake and spoon the dressing round or over the plate and finish off with some chopped dill.

Langustine With Garlic Cream

Prepared langustines (ask fishmonger to prepare)
Garlic
Double cream

Butter
Shallots or finely diced onions

Preheat a deep, heavy based pan and add the butter, finely chopped garlic and onions. Add langustines and sauté over a medium heat for three to four minutes depending on the size of prawns. Keep fluid movement in the pan at all times. Then add cream and reduce sauce to a consistency that coats the back of the spoon. Serve with bread of your choice.

Roasted Chicken Wings

8 chicken wings per person	Mai poy sweet chilli sauce
Celery	Crème fraiche
Carrots	Cashel blue cheese

Place roasting tray on hob. Add a little oil of your choice. Heat oil gently on hob. Add chicken wings and seal them before placing the tray in a preheated oven at 180 deg or 160 fan assisted. Cook chicken thoroughly . Peel celery and carrots. Cut celery and carrots into matchstick sized pieces. To make dressing mix even amounts of crème fraiche and chilli sauce together. Add blue cheese to taste and mix to a combined smooth consistency. To serve – place chicken wings into a bowl with the matchstick vegetables. Add dressing and toss everything together. Make sure the sauce is coating the chicken and vegetables. Serve immediately.

Broccoli, Bacon & Smoked Cheddar Soup

Broccoli	Bacon
Onions	Salt and pepper
Vegetable stock cubes	1 clove of garlic
Good quality smoked Irish cheddar	

Sweat off bacon and onions lightly in a pot until cooked but not coloured. Add the vegetable stock, broccoli and add water. Bring to the boil, reduce heat and simmer for 45 minutes to an hour. To finish, blend the soup in a processor. Add cream to the mixture for consistency and colour. Add grated smoked cheese to suit your pallet.

Smoked Salmon & Irish Brie Crostini

1 packet of smoked salmon	Salad for garnish
Stick of crusty bread or bread of choice	Brie

Slice and toast bread. Remove skin from brie. Place smoked salmon on bread and place brie on top. Put under a grill until the cheese has melted over the salmon.

Sundried Tomato & Basil Brushetta

One stick of crusty bread	Fresh flat leaf parsley
8 medium tomatoes	Olive oil
1 small jar of sundried tomatoes	Salt and pepper
3 red onions	1 small jar of capers

De-seed and finely dice tomatoes. Peel and de-root red onions, finely dice and add to tomatoes. Roughly chop the jar of sundried tomatoes add the oil from the jar of tomatoes. Roughly chop parsley and add to mixture. Add salt and pepper to taste then add oil to bind the mixture. Slice and toast bread. Decorate plate with salad garnish. Place brushetta mixture on to bread and serve.

Melon, Orange & Peach Cocktail

2 galia melons

1 honeydew melon

3 medium oranges (or a tin of orange segments)

Peach schnapps

Prepare melons by cutting in half and de-seeding. Chop into chunks or use Parisian Scoop/melon baller to scoop out the flesh. To prepare the oranges, skin and segment or use a tin of segmented oranges. Mix oranges and melons together. Portion mixture into glass dishes and drizzle with peach schnapps.

French Onion Soup

Onions

Beef stock

Cracked black pepper

Brown sugar

Brandy

Salt

Butter

Peel and finely slice the onions and lightly sweat off until cooked but not coloured. Add cracked black pepper and brown sugar to lightly caramelise. Add beef stock and water, bring to the boil, turn down and simmer until cooked

Dundrum Bay Mussels With Lemongrass & Chilli Broth

Dundrum Bay mussels (cleaned)

Shallots

Red chilli or scotch bonnet

1 bunch of lemongrass

Tomato puree

Seasoning

Fish stock

To make the broth deseed and finely dice chilli, finely dice shallots, take the root off, peel and finely chop lemongrass. Sweat off lemongrass, shallots and chilli in a pan. Add tomato puree to mix. Gently cook out on a low heat for 2-3 minutes. Add fish stock and bring to the boil. Gently simmer for 45 minutes to an hour. To cook mussels – heat up a deep pot until hot but not smoking. Place mussels into the hot pan and cover. Keep the pan moving at all times. When mussels are fully opened remove any that are closed. Strain off some of the juice but keep a small amount back. Add a good ladle full of broth and return to the heat and gently simmer for 3-4 minutes and serve in a bowl. Top with fresh coriander.

Prawn & Apple Open Sandwich Dressed In A Bushille Marie Rose Sauce

Greenland prawns

3 apples

Marie rose sauce

Wheaten bread

Celery

Salad of choice

Defrost prawns under cold running water. Thoroughly strain and gently squeeze out as much water as possible from prawns. Core, quarter and finely slice the apple. Peel and finely slice celery. Add some whiskey to the marie rose sauce. Bind all the ingredients with the marie rose sauce. Serve on wheaten bread with the salad of your choice.

Seared Pigeon Breast On A Bed Of Chard & Carmalised Beetroot

2 locally sourced precleaned pigeon breasts

1 vac pac prepared clean beetroots

Fresh red chard or locally sourced herb of your choice

Brown sugar

Port

Butter

Caramelise beetroot – place brown sugar into a pot. Add water to moisten sugar. Gently simmer until sugar dissolves. At this point add your quartered precooked beetroot and port. You may need to add more sugar or liquid to achieve a consistency to evenly coat the beetroot. Once beetroot is caramelised turn off heat and leave to stand. Pigeon – heat butter and oil in a sauté pan. Place pigeon in the pan over a medium heat. Put pigeon skin side down in pan. Cook until golden brown and turn frequently after that until the pigeon is cooked. Try not to overcook the meat. To finish the dish off, remove pigeon from the pan and leave to rest while you add the caramelised beetroot to the pan. This will mix the juices. Spoon on to plate and place your pigeon breasts skin side up on top.

Savouries

Quick Tuna Pizza

BASE:
1 1/2 oz margarine
1 tsp salt
6 oz self raising flour
3-4 tblsp milk

TOPPING:
1 oz margarine
1 onion, peeled and sliced
7 oz can of tuna fish, drained and mashed
1 tsp dried basil
4 oz grated cheese
2 tomatoes, sliced

For the scone dough base, rub fat into flour and salt. Bind together with milk. Roll lightly to a 20 cm (8 inch) round and place on a greased baking tray. Cooking time 20 minutes, over 220ºC, 425ºF or gas mark 7.
Heat margarine and fry onion until soft. Spread over scone base. Top onions with tuna fish. Mix herbs and cheese together and sprinkle over fish. Top with tomato slices and bake in a hot oven for 15-20 minutes. Serve hot in wedges.

Cornish Pasties

PASTRY:
8 oz plain flour
pinch of salt
4 oz margarine
water to mix

FILLING:
8 oz minced steak
1 tomato, chopped
salt and pepper
1 potato, diced
1 onion, chopped

Make pastry, roll out and cut into rounds. Mix filling together in a bowl, then spoon in the middle of circles. Damp edges with water and seal together. Brush with egg wash or milk. Place on a baking sheet and prick with a fork. Bake at 425ºF for 15 minutes and then at 325ºF for 45-60 minutes.

Spaghetti Alla Carbonara

2 oz butter
½-1 clove of garlic
3 eggs
4 tblsp cream

8 oz grilled bacon
2 oz grated cheese
salt and pepper

Melt butter in pan (mix together eggs, cheese, bacon, garlic and cream) add to pan of melted butter. Cook gently, add parsley and cooked spaghetti.

Kentish Pork *(serves 4)*

4 pork chops
1½ oz butter
1 oz flour
chopped parsley

salt and pepper
1 onion, chopped
¼ pint chicken stock
2 cooking apples

Season chops and gently fry in butter until lightly browned on both sides and cooked through, gently fry onion until soft. Add flour and cook for 1-2 minutes. Blend in stock and milk, bring to the boil, stirring continuously. Add chops and chopped cooking apple and simmer for 15 minutes. Serve chops with remaining apple cut into rings sauted lightly in melted butter. Garnish with chopped parsley. Serve with broccoli and carrots.

Cheese & Bacon Flan

8 oz shortcrust pastry, frozen or a mix will do
FILLING:
2 eggs, beaten
6 oz cheese, grated

1 medium onion, chopped
¼ pint milk
4 rashers of bacon, chopped
seasoning

Roll out pastry and use to line a greased flan ring. Beat the eggs with the milk, add rest of the ingredients and pour into a flan case. Bake in a pre-heated oven at gas mark 4 for 45 minutes or until set. Serve if you like garnished with tomato.

Chicken Curry

1 large chicken
1 small onion
1 tsp chilli
1 tsp powdered ginger
1 tsp mixed spice

2 oz butter
1½ pints chicken stock
1 tsp tumeric
bunch of fresh herbs
1 tsp curry powder

Chop onion and blend with ginger, chilli and turmeric. Fry in butter for several minutes then add the rest of the ingredients and just enough stock to cover. Simmer steadily for about 2 hours and serve with boiled rice and side dishes.

Fried Chicken

1 chicken
1 1/2 oz butter
4 tomatoes (medium)

1 level tsp flour
8 mushrooms
4 potatoes cut in slices

Cut chicken into neat joints and wash. Coat chicken well in seasoned flour. Shallow fry in butter for 15-20 minutes. Add seasoned prepared mushrooms and fry for 7-10 minutes. Add halved seasoned tomatoes and fry for 2-3 minutes. Fry potatoes in deep fat. Serve chicken when tender with mushrooms, tomatoes and potatoes around.

Winter Salad

½ pint boiling water
small tin crushed pineapple
2 oz chopped white celery
1 eating apple, chopped

1 pineapple or lemon jelly
2 oz coarsely grated carrot
1 small onion, chopped

Dissolve jelly in water and allow to cool, add all other ingredients to the jelly when set. Decorate with hard boiled eggs or grapes.

Chicken Pieces - Australian Style

1 chopped onion
3 cloves of garlic, crushed
2 tbsp soy sauce

2 tbsp oil
1 cup vinegar
pinch of salt

Fry garlic and onion until brown, then put in chicken pieces and cook gently turning as they cook. Pour over the vinegar and soy sauce and cook until they are absorbed by the chicken. Season to taste.

Chicken Pie

¾ pint white sauce
1 cooked chicken
½ packet frozen mixed vegetables
1 onion, chopped

salt and pepper
1 cup vinegar
pinch of salt

Cut chicken into small pieces. Chop onion. Add to white sauce and cooked mixed vegetables, season with salt and pepper. Place in an oven proof dish. Combine breadcrumbs and grated cheese and sprinkle on top. Bake in a moderate oven for 30 minutes.

Quick Recipe For Chicken Pie

1 packet bought frozen puff pastry, defrosted
½ cooked chicken, chopped
2-4 oz cooked carrots
4 oz frozen peas, cooked

1 onion, sliced and fried
1 packet Knorr Cream of Chicken soup
1 large square dish or large round casserole dish

Make up soup according to the recipe on the packet. Add the chopped chicken, cooked carrots, cooked peas and onion. Put into dish, roll out puff pastry and cover filling. Pierce pastry on top with a skewer or fork. Bake in an oven at 180-200ºC for 30-40 minutes until pastry is golden, serve hot.

Beef Strogonoff *(serves 4)*

1 lb topside
1 small onion
seasoned flour
1 can condensed Cream of Mushroom soup

1 small can tomato puree
1 small carton cream
½ lb mushrooms

Cut meat into half inch cubes and toss in seasoned flour. Place in casserole along with finely chopped onion, cook until brown. Add mushroom soup and small can of tomatoes, then add sliced mushrooms. Place in oven at 180ºC, 360ºF for 45-60 minutes. Stir in cream just before serving. Serve on a bed of rice or pasta.

Steak Parcels

4 portions sirloin, fillet or chump steak
4 oz mushrooms, chopped
1 medium onion, chopped

4 small tomatoes, chopped
salt and pepper
chopped parsley to garnish

Heat a little oil in pan and brown steaks on each side, about one minute per side. Then add mushrooms, onion and tomato, cook for a few minutes. Cut 4 squares of tinfoil to wrap around each steak. Divide mixture over top of each steak, season and wrap in foil. Complete cooking on a moderate oven, underdone for about 30 minutes or well done for approximately one hour. Time depends on the steak used. Excellent when entertaining as they don't require any attention while cooking and can be prepared in advance.

Beef Hotpot

12 oz-1 lb (300 g-400 g) lean braising steak
1 7 oz (175 g) tin whole kernel sweetcorn, drained
seasoned flour
1 oz (25 g) dripping (or similar)

4 carrots, sliced
3 potatoes, peeled and sliced
1 level tsp (5 ml) made mustard
½ pint (250 ml) stock

Toss the meat in the seasoned flour and brown in the hot fat. Lift from the pan and place in a 2 pint casserole dish. Add the carrots, potatoes, mustard and stock to the meat. Season (if necessary) and cover with a lid. Place in the centre of a moderate oven and cook for 2-2 ½ hours. Add the sweetcorn and cook for a further 15 minutes, then serve with crusty French bread and butter.

Cheese, Bacon & Tomato Flan

6 oz plain flour	2-3 slices of bacon
4 oz margarine	1 tomato
pinch of salt	2 oz cheese, grated
1 egg and a little water	little milk
5 large eggs	salt

Preheat oven to 200ºC. 1 medium flan dish or deep pie dish (greased) Rub margarine into flour, add salt. Bind with beaten egg and a little water to make a firm dough. Roll out pastry case and line greased dish. Pierce pastry with a fork. Pre-cook pastry case in oven for 10 minutes or until light golden in colour. Remove from oven and add filling. Five large eggs beaten with a little milk added, add pinch salt, grated cheese. Pour into pastry case, cover with slices of bacon on top with sliced tomato and sprinkle with a little grated cheese.

Pizza Ricci *(5 portions)*

BASE:	FILLING:
6 oz self rising flour	2 tins tomatoes, drained and chopped
1 egg and a little milk	3 oz mushrooms, sliced and fried lightly together with
2 oz margarine (block or soft)	2 sliced medium onions
3 dsp oregano	2-3 slices cooked ham, chopped
pinch of salt	2 oz grated cheddar cheese
1 large flat bottomed square roasting tin (greased)	2 fresh tomatoes, sliced
	(optional - chopped pineapple if liked)

Preheat oven to 200ºC. Put flour into a bowl, rub in the margarine, add oregano and salt, bind together with egg and milk. Roll out into a round (not too thick). Cook in oven for 15 minutes till golden. Remove from oven and cover with chopped tomatoes then mushrooms and onions. Then chop ham, finely sliced tomatoes and sprinkle with grated cheese. (If adding pineapple,, add it along with the ham). Put into the oven again and cook for a further 20 minutes. Remove and slice.

Pork Chops Italiano

pork chops	2-4 oz mushrooms
1 small onion	1 small pepper
small tin of cream of tomato soup (or packet)	bay leaf

Trim chops and season. Brown on both sides and remove from pan. Add onion and cook gently until tender and lightly brown. Replace chops and add soup, mushrooms, green pepper and lemon juice. Cover and simmer gently for 1 hour. Serve chops with the sauce poured over accompanied with creamed potatoes and green beans.

Sweet & Sour Sausage Pie

1 lb sausages	3 medium sliced potatoes
3 large tomatoes	knob of butter
2 hard boiled eggs	seasoning
2 large cooking apples	1 oz brown sugar

Skin sausages, split in half and place a layer in pie dish. Skin and slice tomatoes and place on top of sausages. Add a layer of hard boiled egg and season. Add a layer of sliced apple and sprinkle with brown sugar. Continue with alternate layers until the dish is filled. Lastly place a layer of sliced par-boiled potatoes and dab with knobs of butter. Cover with foil and cook in a moderate oven. Remove foil about ½ hour before serving to allow top to brown slightly.

Grilled Gammon Steak With Marmalade Sauce

4 gammon steaks	1 small chopped onion
4 tblsp marmalade	2 tsp white wine vinegar
10 oz demerara sugar	

Pre-heat moderate grill. Remove rind and snip fat at intervals. Put steaks into a large bowl and cover with boiling water. Leave for 5 minutes. Drain and brush with oil. Place steaks on grill rack, and cook gently for 15 minutes turning once. Place onions in a small saucepan with 1 tsp of oil, cook without browning for 5 minutes. Stir in the marmalade, vinegar and sugar. Beat gently to dissolve. Bring to the boil and reduce to a syrup-type sauce. Place gammon on serving dish and cover with the sauce.

Sweet & Sour Pork

1½ lb pieces of pork fillet
seasoned flour (to cover pork)
½ tblsp Worcestershire sauce
1 tsp salt
½ pint chicken stock
3½ oz can pineapple pieces
2 tblsp mango chutney
1 tblsp wine vinegar

½ tblsp soy sauce
1 large finely chopped onion
1 tsp oil
2 tblsp tomato puree or tomato ketchup
1 tsp honey
3½ oz tin pimentos *
1 small green pepper*

*Cut pork into neat pieces, removing excess fat. Toss in seasoned flour, fry in a heavy pan in hot fat till nicely browned. Remove from pan. Add a little more oil if necessary. Fry onion until soft and slightly brown. Stir in 2 tblsp flour, add rest of ingredients for the sauce. Add sliced green peper and sliced pimento. Bring to boil and cook on gentle heat for approximately 1½ hours till pork is tender. This can be cooked on top of the cooker or in the oven. Oven 350ºF, 180ºC, gas mark 4. Serve in a casserole dish accompanied by a dish of boiled rice. *optional*

Savoury Mince & Mushroom Pie

1 lb mince steak
1 onion

¼ lb mushrooms
2 packets cheese and onion crisps

Fry mince and onion until browned. Drain off excess fat and add chopped mushrooms. Cover and cook for 30 minutes. Add one packet of crushed crisps and cool slightly. Make shortcrust pastry using 6 oz plain flour and 3 oz margarine. Line a swiss roll tin with pastry and bake blind. Spread meat over pastry then crush packet of crisps and sprinkle over top, return to oven and heat through.

Cheese & Marrow Savoury

1 or 2 young marrows
1 oz butter
4 tomatoes
seasoning

8 oz grated cheese
1 level tsp flour
½ gill water

Slice marrow into rings. Take out seeds but do not remove peel if very young. Sprinkle with salt. Steam over boiling water until tender. Meanwhile, fry sliced tomatoes in butter. Blend flour with water, add to tomato mixture and cook until thick, but smooth. Stir in 6 oz cheese and seasoning. Arrange marrow rings on dish, cover with cheese mixture. Sprinkle with grated cheese and brown under grill or in oven. Serve with young vegetables.

Savoury Beef with Macaroni

1 lb minced beef
1 oz butter
2 oz mushrooms
7 oz tin of tomatoes
½ pint white coating sauce

1 onion
¼ tsp basil
¼ tsp oregano
3 oz macaroni, cooked
2 oz grated cheese

Melt butter, fry onions, add minced beef and cook till browned. Add herbs, chopped mushrooms and tomatoes, simmer for 5-10 minutes. Stir in cooked macaroni and place mixture in an ovenproof casserole. Make up ½ pint white sauce and immediately stir in half of the cheese, cover meat mixture with the sauce and sprinkle over the remaining cheese. Bake in a moderately hot oven for 20 minutes.

Chicken In Sweet & Sour Sauce

8 chicken drumsticks
2 tsp powdered ginger
2 tblsp cornflour
5 tblsp vinegar
3-4 tblsp brown sugar
11 oz can pineapple pieces
1 red pepper, seeded and sliced

salt and freshly ground black pepper
1 oz butter for grilling
cold water
2 tsp soya sauce
½ piint chicken stock
4 tomatoes, skinned and quartered

Cooking time - 30 minutes. Oven 180ºC, 350ºF, gas mark 4. Season chicken with salt and pepper. Rub ginger into surface of each joint and dot each with a knob of butter. Grill until golden and transfer to casserole dish. In a pan blend cornfour with a little cold water, stir in vinegar, soya sauce, sugar and chicken stock. Bring slowly to the boil stirring until sauce thickens, stir in pineapple pieces and juice, tomatoes and red pepper. Pour sauce over joints and cover. Serve with boiled rice.

Sweet & Sour Pork

2 lb pork fillet
1 tblsp soya sauce
1-2 onions, sliced
3 oz soft brown sugar
1 tsp cornflour to thicken

12 can pineapple chunks
4 tblsp vinegar
1-2 green peppers, de-seeded and sliced
pinch of salt

Cut the pork fillet into cubes and fry until brown. Drain the pineapples into a measuring jug and make the liquid up to ½ pint with water. Add the vinegar and soya sauce. Put the sliced onions, peppers and pineapples into a casserole. Add the soft brown sugar and the juice. Simmer and thicken with cornflour. Add the pork and cook for 1 ½ hours at 2240ºF, 120ºC, gas mark ½.

Kedgeree

500 g fish (salmon, haddock or smoked)
250 g patma rice
50 g margarine
salt

curry powder
2 hard boiled eggs
lemon and parsley for garnish

Wash and dry fish, poach or steam until tender. Drain and flake, removing bones and skin. Wash rice and place in boiling water and salt. Boil for 10-12 minutes until cooked. Drain and pour poiling water through and drain again. Melt margarine in a pan and re-heat rice and haddock by tossing in margarine. Season and add curry powder to taste. Chop one egg and add to fish, slice second egg for garnish. Serve on an oval dish, garnish with egg, lemon and parsley. This dish may be served hot or cold.

Salmon Pie

1 cup of rice
1 tin condensed mushroom soup
½ tin milk

1 7oz tin salmon
potato crisps

Boil rice and grease oven-proof dish, drain salmon and remove bones. Put boiled rice into dish and add salmon, flake it through and add juice, soup and milk. Mix well and season. Cover with crushed potato crisps. Put into pre-heated oven for 35-40 minutes, 325°-350°.

Golden Plaice

4 medium fillets of plaice
½ oz (15 g) margarine
juice and rind of 1 orange

STUFFING:
small tin of corn niblets
1 green pepper
4 oz (100 g) cottage cheese
1 orange, peeled
pepper and salt

STUFFING: Chop half the orange and half the pepper. Mix with corn niblets, cheese etc. Divide between the fillets of plaice and roll up. Put into ovenproof dish and dot with margarine. Add juice and rind of first orange. Cover and cook for 40 minutes at 375°F, 190°C, gas mark 4. Garnish with remaining orange and pepper.

Pork & Pineapple Casserole

small tin of pineapple chunks
small stick of celery (optional)
small eating apple
½ lb streaky bacon
1 tblsp cornflour

1 lb pork pieces
small onion, chopped
¼ lb mushrooms
1 tsp tomato ketchup

Brown pork and bacon in a pan and place into casserole. Drain pineapple pieces and add into casserole. Make pineapple juice up to 2 fl oz with water. Add 1 tblsp of cornflour to liquid. Mix and pour over pork and vegetables. Add tomato ketchup and mix. Cook and cover at 150ºC, 300ºF for 2 hours and serve with rice.

Fish & Tomato Casserole

½ lb fish
few tomatoes , sliced
2 oz grated cheese

parsley, chopped finely
1 onion, chopped finely
2 oz breadcrumbs

Put fish into casserole dish. Sprinkle with salt and pepper. Place tomatoes, onion and parsley into a pan and simmer for 10-15 minutes. Add to fish once simmered. Mix cheese and breadcrumbs and sprinkle on top. Decorate with parsley. Cook in oven at 180ºC, 360ºF for 30 minutes.

Chicken Casserole

1 chicken or chicken pieces
1 small tin pineapple rings
breadcrumbs

½ lb mushrooms
1 egg

Portion chicken and remove skin. Dip each portion in beaten egg. Roll in breadcrumbs and fry until golden. Place in casserole dish with mushrooms and place pineapple rings on top and 2 tblsp of pineapple juice over contents of dish. Serve with French fried potatoes or mashed potatoes. Cook for 1 hour at 230ºC or 450ºF.

Devilled Lamb

4 lamb chops
1 tsp Worcester sauce
pinch of curry powder

1 tblsp chopped parsley
2 oz butter

Put chops under hot grill and brown well on one side. Turn and cook for one minute on other side. Blend butter, parsley, sauce and curry powder. Spread over hot chops and cook steadily for about 8 minutes under the grill.

Spaghetti Bolognaise

30 g (1 oz) butter
2 medium onions
470 g (150 oz) can whole tomatoes
1 tsp basil
½ tsp thyme
1 clove of garlic, crushed
grated Parmesan cheese

2 tblsp oil
750 g (1½ lb) minced steak
3 tblsp tomato puree
1 tsp oregano
salt and pepper
1.25 litres water

Heat oil in large frying pan, add peeled and chopped onions. Saute gently until onions are tender, add minced steak, stir over a high heat until meat is dark golden brown, mashing meat well. Add undrained tomatoes, tomato puree, basil, oregano and thyme, mix well. Season with salt and pepper. Add water and two chicken cubes. Bring to boil, reduce heat and simmer uncovered for two hours until nearly all liquid has evaporated. Serve with Parmesan cheese.

Hot Pot

1½ lb middle neck lamb chops
1½ oz margarine
2 onions, sliced
pinch of salt
black pepper

1 tsp mixed herbs
1 chicken stock cube, crumbled with 1 tsp flour
8 oz can chopped tomatoes
1½ lb peeled and sliced potatoes
2nd chicken stock cube dissolved in ⅓ pint hot water

Trim chops and toss in flour and crumbled stock cube mixture. Melt 1 oz of margarine in frying pan. Fry meat quickly on both sides for 2-3 minutes and place in a casserole dish. Fry onions for 5 minutes or until soft, then add tinned tomatoes, herbs, seasonings. Mix well and add to meat. Parboil the potatoes for five minutes, drain well before layering the slices carefully on top of the meat. Stir any remaining flour into the frying pan for one minute, then add the chicken stock. Bring to the boil and pour liquid over the potatoes so it runs through to the meat. Dot the remaining margarine on the potatoes. Cover with a lid and place the dish in the centre of a moderately hot oven for about an hour. Then remove the lid and bake for a further half an hour to allow potatoes to brown.

Country Lamb Casserole

2 lb best end of neck of lamb
1 lb carrots, scraped and chopped
salt and freshly ground black pepper
1½ pints boiling water

8 oz onions, peeled and sliced
1½ lb potatoes, peeled and thickly sliced
½ tsp dried thyme
chopped parsley to finish

Cut neck into chops and season well. Put alternative layers of vegetables and meat in a large casserole dish and finish with a layer of potato, season well between the layers and sprinkle the herbs at the same time. Pour the water over the meat, cover and cook in a slow oven at 170ºC, 325ºF, gas mark 3 for about 2 hours. Just before serving skim and sprinkle well with parsley. Serve with buttered cabbage.

Lamb Crumble

2 oz (50 g) butter
2 oz (50 g) crumbled cheese
12 oz (325/350 g) cold roast lamb
2 level tblsp tomato puree
½ pint stock

4½ oz (120 g) sifted flour
½ level tsp mixed herbs
salt and pepper
3 oz (75 g) onions
1 level tblsp cornflour

Rub butter finely into 4 oz flour, add cheese, herbs and seasoning, mince meat and onion together. Stir in remaining ingredients. Slowly bring to boil. Place into a pie dish and cover with crumble. Bake at gas mark 5 for 45 minutes to 1 hour.

Grilled Lamb Cutlets

4 lamb cutlets or lamb chops
2 large/4 small skinned sausages or 4 oz sausage meat
2 tsp chopped parsley
stuffing

tsp grated lemon rind
1 egg yolk
pinch of mixed herbs and seasoning

Cooking time 15 minutes. Mix ingredients for stuffing together. Cut the meat away from the bone for 2-3 inches. Press stuffing into the cavity making it flat and neat. Put the stuffed chops under the grill, cook on both sides until crisp and brown. Serve with potato crisps, grilled tomatoes, peas and watercress.

Chicken Stuffed With Sundried Tomato & Basil Pesto In Parma Ham

4 8oz skin on chicken fillets
I packet of good quality Parma ham
1 jar of basil pesto

1 jar of sundried tomato pesto
breadcrumbs

Place chicken breasts on a chopping board skin side down. MOVE INNER FILLET TO ITS NATURAL position. With a fillet knife make a pocket at the top end of the fillet (a small incision) Mix together the pesto in a bowl, add breadcrumbs to thicken pesto. Roll the stuffing into balls and place inside the pocket you have made in the chicken. Cover the incision with the inner fillet and in a hot pan seal the chicken. Place in a preheated over 180°C. Cook for 12-15 minutes. Remove from oven. On a clean chopping board place out slices of Parma ham. Wrap the chicken fillet in the Parma ham and return to hob until the ham is gold and crisp. Serve with a fresh salad of your choice.

Minted Pepper Lamb Rump

4 8-10 oz lamb rump steak
packet of mint or a jar of mint sauce (preferably fresh mint)

cracked black pepper
salt to taste
Olive oil

Score the lamb making a diamond shape without breaking the layer of fat. Marinade – if using fresh mint, chop, if not two tablespoons of mint sauce. Cracked black pepper and salt. Mix with olive oil. Place meat and the marinade in a container and leave for four hours, preferably overnight. Remove meat from marinade and sear in a hot pan and cook to your liking in the oven. Serve with champ and if required a sauce of your own choice. Recommendations – redcurrant jus or rosemary jus.

Paddy Pizza

soda farls
jar of tomato sauce (dolmeo etc)
smoked bacon

mushrooms
cheese

Slice bacon and mushrooms and grate the cheese. Cut soda in half evenly. Spread tomato sauce onto the soda bread. Place the precooked sliced bacon and mushrooms on top of that. Top with grated cheese. Place in a preheated oven at 200ºC 180ºC fan assisted oven until cheese is melted and golden. (alternative toppings can be used) Serve on its own or with salad.

Medallions of Fillet Steak in a Madeira Sauce

4 10oz fillet steaks
madeira
double cream

salt and pepper
beef stock

Cut the fillet steak into three even pieces. Season the beef with salt and pepper before cooking. Cook the steak to your own taste. In a pot flambé the alcohol off the madeira, add beef stock, cream and reduce to consistency of coating the back of spoon. Season to taste. Serve with flavoured mash or other sides of your own choice.

Barbary Duck Fillet With Maranello Cherry Jus

duck fillets
tinned maranello cherries
1 jar of redcurrant jelly
vegetable stock
brandy

butter
oil
salt and pepper
flat leaf parsley to garnish

To prepare duck. Remove from package and score fat without breaking into the flesh. Preheat pan with butter and oil on a medium heat in an ovenproof pan. Seal the duck in the pan, skin side down first, cook in the oven to medium rare or medium for 15 minutes at 200ºC. Sauce – remove duck from pan and leave to rest. To the juice of the pan deglaze with the brandy and cook off alcohol. Add cherries and redcurrant jelly, salt and pepper to taste. Reduce sauce until it coats the back of a spoon. To serve – slice duck diagonally and arrange on plate, spoon sauce over.

Slow Roasted Pork Fillet

pork fillet (ask your butcher to prepare fillet by clearing sinew and access fat)
1 large or 2 small cooking apples
6 shallots

double cream
vegetable stock
salt and pepper
brown sugar

To cook the pork, place roasting dish on hob with a little oil. Sear the pork fillet. Place in a preheated oven at 150 or 130 fan assisted. Cook pork until juices run clear and the meat is cooked through (time depends on size of fillet). To prepare the sauce finely slice the shallots, peel, decore and finely slice the cooking apples. Fry off the shallots for 2-3 minutes until they are soft but not coloured. Add sugar, diced apples and a vegetable stock cube and a little liquid until the mixture is covered. Gently simmer until sugar is dissolved but not caramelised. Add the cream to the juice and cook until it has reached the consistency of coating the back of a spoon. Serve – slice pork at an angle into 2-3 inch pieces. Arrange on plate. Spoon sauce over the meat. Serve with roasted new Comber potatoes.

Seared Fillet Of Salmon With Ginger, Chilli & Soy Dressing

4 lamb shanks
soup vegetable mix
red wine
redcurrant jelly

oil
flour
rosemary

Dressing – finely chop the ginger, chillies and scallions. Add the honey, soy sauce and oil. Coat skin side of salmon lightly in flour. Sear both sides of the salmon in a preheated hot pan. Finish in oven for 12-15 minutes at 180ºC fan assisted. Serve with side order of choice. Spoon dressing around plate.

Braised Lamb Shank

8 oz salmon fillets
ginger
fresh chillies
scallions

soy sauce
olive oil
honey

Coat lamb shanks in flour and cook in a large pan until sealed. Take pan off the heat and leave to rest. Sweat off vegetables and rosemary in a deep roasting tray on the hob along with the herbs. Once sweated off add redcurrant jelly and wine. Place lamb shanks in the mixture ensuring they are sitting on the bed of vegetables and not touching the tray. The lamb shanks must then be covered with the stock. Place in a preheated oven at 130ºC fan assisted for three hours turning halfway through. To make gravy – strain off juice, add some tomato puree and reduce. If gravy needs thickened use cornflour.

Crusted Panfried Trout With Lemon & Caper Butter

trout fillets (ask fishmonger to prepare)	butter
eggs	capers
flour	lemon
porridge oats	

Coating trout – Make egg wash (beat egg and milk together). Lightly flour the trout fillets. Place into the egg wash and then into a bowl of dried porridge oats. You may need to repeat these two steps again if the fish is not coated thoroughly. Preheat a pan to a medium heat. Place the fillets in the pan. Seal both sides of the fillets before reducing heat to low. Turn occasionally until the trout is cooked thoroughly.

Caper Butter - Soften butter until room temperature. Mix capers with butter after the capers have been strained off from juice. Add zest of a lemon and the juice of half a lemon. Mix together and place on a sheet of greaseproof paper and roll into a log and place into the fridge or freezer to set. Serve – With a knob of caper butter and side of your own choice.

Pan Fried Chicken Fillet with Tagliatelle & Prawn Cream

8oz skin on fillets	garlic
small bag of frozen prawns	shallots
fresh tagliatelle	dill
double cream	

Seal chicken in a hot pan. Place pan in a 180ºC oven for 15 minutes. Sauce – Defrost the prawns. Keep a quarter of the prawns to the side for garnish. Finely slice the shallots. Chop garlic. Sweat off shallots and garlic and add cream. Then add prawns and reduce. Blend the sauce using a food processor or hand blender. Pasta – cook pasta. To serve- mix the prawn sauce with the pasta. Add the leftover prawns and gently fold in without damaging the pasta or prawns. In a pasta bowl place the pasta mixture. Top that with the diagonally sliced chicken. Sprinkle with chopped dill and cheese of choice (optional).

Minted Lamb Koftas

minced lamb	egg yolk
shallots or onions	flour
fresh mint	salt and pepper
salt and pepper	

Finely dice the shallots or onions and roughly chop the mint. Add the onions and mint to the minced lamb. Bind together using the yolk of the egg. Lightly season the mix. Mould the mix into burger shaped patties. Lightly coat in flour. Seal all sides of the patties in a medium heated pan but do not brown. Place patties in a preheated oven at 200ºC or 180ºC fan assisted oven until thoroughly cooked. Serve in a bun or with a side salad of your choice.

Chicken Fajhita

chicken breasts

cooking oil

onions

peppers

flour tortillas

cajun seasoning

jar of tomato based salsa

On a medium heat place diced chicken or chicken strips into a pan with hot oil. Keep movement in the pan fluid to stop chicken from sticking. When chicken is sealed add dry Cajun mix and continue to cook whilst keeping fluid movement for a further two to three minutes on a medium heat. At this point add sliced onions and peppers and cook until vegetables are soft. Then add jar of salsa . Place floured tortillas under a low heated grill or a cool oven 100°C until they are warm but retain their softness. Spoon the mix into the middle of the wrap and fold the wrap. Serve with salad or side order of your choice.

Sweet Chilli Beef Stir Fry With Egg Noodles

strips of beef

onions

peppers

mushrooms

tin of water chestnuts

optional – beansprouts

May Poi chilli sauce

beef stock cube

noodles

Fry off beef in a hot wok. When the beef is coloured add the vegetables (finely sliced). When the vegetables are cooked add a beef stock cube and some water, chilli sauce and toss cooked noodles through the dish straight away. When steam rises off noodles dish is ready to serve.

Vegetable Lasagne

onions

courgettes

aubergines

peppers

mushrooms

baby corn

carrots

jar of white sauce

jar of tomato sauce

vegetable stock

oil

salt and pepper

sheets of lasagne

tomato puree

garlic

cheese

Prepare vegetables by cutting into even sized chunks or strips. Sweat off vegetables in a pan on a medium heat until they are soft but not coloured. Add seasoning, vegetable stock cubes, garlic, tomato puree whilst continually stirring as it is easy to burn tomato puree. Keep on medium heat for two to three minutes. Add the tomato sauce and bring to a gentle simmer and turn off heat. White sauce - Mustard or herb of choice can be added to the jar of sauce to add depth and flavour. Lightly coat the bottom of the casserole dish with the white sauce. Place an even layer of lasagne sheets on to this. On top of this put an even layer of the tomato and vegetable mix. On top of that place another layer of lasagne sheets followed by another layer of white sauce. On top of that place another layer of lasagne sheets to which you add another layer of the tomato and vegetable mix, another layer of lasagne sheets with a generous covering of white sauce and cheese of your choice. Bake in oven at 200°C fan assisted 180°C until golden brown and soft to the touch with a knife and lasagne is cooked through.

Sides

Honey Roasted Root Vegetables

carrots

parsnips

shallots

and other alternative root vegetables

honey

oil

seasoning

Blanch the vegetables before placing on to a hot roasting tray thoroughly coating in oil, seasoning and honey. Roast in an oven at 200ºC for 20-25 minutes. Serve with garnish.

Roasted New Comber Potatoes

new Comber baby potatoes

oil

salt and pepper

rosemary

Par boil potatoes until just cooked. Then place in a hot roasting tray with rosemary, oil and seasoning. Coat thoroughly and roast in a hot oven until golden brown.

Wholegrain Mustard & Armagh Apple Mash

potatoes

milk

butter

wholegrain mustard

apple

salt and pepper

Boil potatoes. Strain and thoroughly drain of water. Return to a low heat until the butter has melted. Mash, season and add the diced apple and wholegrain mustard to taste.

Bubble & Squeak Potato Cake

savoy cabbage

smoked bacon lardons

potatoes

salt and pepper

milk

butter

flour

Make mash using potatoes. Add cooked bacon lardons and savoy cabbage. Mix thoroughly and place into a shallow two inch flan dish. Allow to cool and then cover with cling film and weigh down in fridge. Cut out cakes with pastry cutter. Lightly coat the cake in flour and fry in a hot pan until the outside of the cake is brown. Finish off in an oven preheated at 200ºC for five minutes or until thoroughly heated.

Carrot & Coriander Puree

carrots	salt
coriander	pepper
double cream	butter

Peel and thickly slice carrots. Boil carrots in vegetable stock. Strain off carrots and mash. Add chopped coriander, salt and pepper to the mash. Place mash in food processor and add a small amount of cream. Blitz until mixture forms a puree. For extra smoothness pass through sieve

Medley Of Green Vegetables

savoy cabbage	butter
french beans	salt and pepper
sugar snap peas	chicken stock
garden peas	diced onions

Fry off diced onions and finely shredded Savoy cabbage. Add the chicken stock, cover and reduce heat for five minutes. Prior to serving add sugar snap peas, French beans and garden peas. Heat through, season and serve.
Optional - smoked bacon can be added to enhance flavour of dish

Sweets & Puddings

Butterscotch Pie

3 oz shortcrust pastry	1 teacup brown sugar
4 tblsp water	1 teacup milk
1 egg	2 oz margarine
4 level tsp flour	

Mix sugar, flour and blend with water. Boil milk and pour over. Then return to saucepan, add margarine. Cook slowly until thick. Cool and add egg yolk and flavouring. Pour into pastry case and pile meringue on top.

Rhubarb Mousse

1 lb rhubarb	2 oz sugar
1 strawberry jelly	2 oz butter
2 eggs	1 tblsp jam

Cut up rhubarb and stew slowly with sugar. Add strawberry jelly (broken up) then butter. Cool and put in a blender. Add egg yolks and strawberry jam, blend all. Whip egg white stiffly and fold into mixture.

Pear Meringue

1 large tin of pears	2 packets custard powder
1 pint of milk	2 eggs
3-4 tblsp sugar	

Grease pie dish. Chop pears into chunks and place at bottom of dish. Make a fairly thick custard with the milk, pear juice and the 2 tblsp sugar and the egg yolks. Pour over pears, leave to cool. Whip the 2 egg whites into peaks, then add 4 oz castor sugar. Cover the custard with meringue and cook until set about 180ºC.

Chocolate Krispie Cream

4 oz chocolate	small carton whipping cream
4 oz Mars Bars	2 egg whites
2 oz butter	3 oz castor sugar
3 oz Rice Krispies	

Melt Mars Bars and butter in a saucepan. Pour in Rice Krispies. Use to make a flan base, allow to cool. Whip egg whites until stiff then add sugar. Melt chocolate. Whip cream and combine all three together and pour into flan.

Lime Cheesecake

BASE:
6 oz digestive biscuits, crushed
2 oz castor sugar
2 oz margarine

FILLING:
1 lemon
1 lime jelly
1 packet dream topping
1 small packet Philadelphia cheese

BASE: Cream margarine and sugar and add crumbs. Press into a cake tin (one with a loose bottom). Cook for 10 minutes at gas mark 2, cool.
TOPPING: Melt jelly in ½ pint water, add juice and rind of lemon. Leave till cold. Beat dream topping, add cheese and jelly and beat all together. Pour on top of cold base. Leave in fridge to set, decorate with fresh cream.

Black Forest Trifle

Sprinkle trifle sponge with sherry, cover with cherry pie filling and thick custard. When cool, top with whipped cream and cherries and grated chocolate.

Lemon Fridge Cake

2 packets biscuits
4 lemons
lemon rind

2 14 oz (350 g) full cream
condensed milk
2 15 oz (375 g) ready to serve custard, hot

Using a 9 by 11 inch serving dish, put layer of biscuits and cover with hot custard. Put second layer of biscuits on top. Whisk condensed milk in large bowl. Grate lemons and add juice to milk. Whisk thoroughly. Pour over biscuits and sprinkle with grated rind. Put in fridge until cold. Serve with whipped cream.

Pineapple Cheesecake

1 small tin crushed pineapples
2 oz margarine
5 oz digestive biscuits, crushed

2 oz castor sugar
½ pint fresh cream
small packet Philadelphia cheese

BASE: Melt margarine and crushed biscuits and sugar. Put into flan dish and press well down.
TOPPING: Cream Philadelphia cheese and 2 oz castor sugar together. Drain pineapples. Whip cream until stiff and combine together with cheese and pineapples. Put on top of biscuit base, smooth out and place in fridge to set.

Black Forest Pudding

4 oz brown breadcrumbs
6 level tblsp drinking chocolate
1 tin cherry pie filling
2 tsp instant coffee

4 oz demerara sugar
½ pint single cream
1 chocolate flake

Mix together pie filling, breadcrumbs, sugar, drinking chocolate and coffee. Add some Kirsch or cherry brandy, whip cream until thick. Coat sides of a glass serving dish with cream and layer mixture and cream into dish, finishing with a layer of cream. Top with crushed chocolate flake. Leave in fridge overnight.

Banana Crumble

5 ripe bananas
8 oz self raising flour
3 tblsp water

1½ lb sugar
4 oz margarine
6 oz sugar

Peel bananas and roughly slice into a large buttered casserole dish, then sprinkle over them the sugar and water. Rub margarine into flour until it resembles fine breadcrumbs then add the sugar. Sprinkle the crumb mixture over bananas. Bake in a moderately hot oven for about 25 minutes until golden brown. Serve hot with cream or custard.

Pavlova

4 egg whites
1 tsp white vinegar
1 tblsp cornflour

6 oz castor sugar
2 oz icing sugar

Put four egg whites into a mixing bowl, beat till stiff. Add 6 oz castor sugar and 2 oz icing sugar. Beat until fluffy and glossy. Add 1 tblsp of cornflour (sifted) beat again, then fold in 1 tsp of white vinegar. Pile mixture on to a tin foil covered plate and bake at 150° for 1 hour, then turn your oven down to 100°C and bake for a further hour. Leave overnight or a few hours in fridge. When cool cover with whipped cream and fruit salad.

Pavlova

4 egg whites
4 dsp cold water

8 oz castor sugar
tsp vanilla essence

Put everything in a bowl and beat for 8 minutes. Line tin with greaseproof paper oiled. Rinse greaseproof paper under tap, shake off excess water. Bake at 300°F for 40 minutes. Turn off oven and leave in oven until cool. Serve with fresh cream, fresh raspberries, strawberries or another fruit.

Tasmanian Pudding

2-4 oz castor sugar	1 teacup milk
2 tblsp plain flour	2 eggs
2 oz margarine	1 lemon

Cream margarine and sugar, add well beaten egg yolk. Stir in flour and milk. Add juice and rind of lemon. Fold in stiffly beaten egg whites. Pour into greased pie dish and place in a larger dish of cold water. Bake in moderate oven for 30 minutes until brown.

Mixed Fruit & Coconut Crumble

1 lb mixed fruit (cooking apples, plums & blackberries)	6 oz plain flour
2 tblsp demerara sugar	2 oz museli (Alpen)
3 oz margarine	1 tblsp coconut

Put fruit in ovenproof dish, sprinkle sugar over fruit. Rub margarine into flour, add other ingredients, spread over fruit. Bake for 40-45 minutes until lightly browned. Oven 350ºF, 180ºC, gas mark 4. Serve with custard.

Ice Cream Sponge

½ sponge sandwich	small block of ice cream
raspberry jam	¼ pint fresh cream
½ lb grapes	

Split sponge in half and on half spread a layer of raspberry jam and a layer of ice cream. Sandwich together and top with fresh cream, decorate with grapes. Put in the fridge until ready to serve.

Baked Alaska

1 sponge or sandwich	3 eggs
3 oz castor sugar	tsp granulated sugar
plain or ripple ice cream	

MERINGUE TOPPING: Put egg whites into clean, dry bowl, beat until stiff and peaky. Gently fold in castor sugar with large metal spoon. Pile meringue over pie or pudding, etc. and sprinkle with granulated sugar. Flash bake at top of the oven, gas mark 8, until meringue just turning gold, about 1-3 minutes, but no longer. Put sponge or sandwich (7 inch at least 1 day old) on to a heat proof plate, make meringue topping. Put tblsp of ice cream in mounds on top of cake, swirl meringue completely over cake and ice cream then flash bake, serve immediately.

Malakoff Dessert *(serves 6-8)*

8 oz fresh or tinned strawberries
4 oz butter
3 oz castor sugar
3 oz ground almonds

5 fl oz cream
6 tblsp orange juice
24 sponge fingers
cream & flaked almonds for decoration

Line a 1½ pint loaf tin with lightly greased greaseproof paper. Cream sugar and butter until pale and fluffy. Beat in the almonds. Gradually stir the cream into the almond mixture. Arrange a layer of sponge fingers in the base of the tin. Sprinkle the fingers with 2 tblsp of juice. Half the strawberries (reserving 8 for decoration). Arrange half of the strawberry halves upon the fingers. Carefully cover the layer of strawberries with ½ the almond mixture. Repeat, i.e. sponge fingers, strawberries and almond mixture. Finish with layer of sponge fingers. Chill until firm (6 hours approximately). Turn on to a serving plate, remove paper and decorate. Can be frozen.

Preserves

Marmalade

2 lb marmalade oranges | 1 lemon
4 lb sugar | 4 pints water

Cut oranges and lemon in half and squeeze out juice. Take out some pith and inside segments, slice finely. Put sliced oranges and lemon into a pan with juice in water. Simmer for 1 hour. Add warmed sugar, boil for 10 minutes or until thickened. Put into heated jars.

Blackcurrant Jam

3 lb blackcurrants | 5 lb sugar
3½ lb jam pots of water |

Remove stalks from blackcurrants. Rinse with cold water. Put fruit and water into a pan and bring to the boil. Boil quickly for exactly 15 minutes, add sugar, dissolve and bring back to the boil again for 15-20 minutes. Not a bit of tough skin or hardness remains, only a smooth richly flavoured preserve, which will keep the year round. Yields about 10 lbs jam.

Gooseberry Jam

4½ lb gooseberries | 1½ pints water
2 kg granulated sugar |

Top and tail fruit and wash. Put into large pan with water. Simmer for 20-30 minutes until skins are tender. Add sugar. Dissolve over a gentle heat. Bring to rolling boil for 10-12 minutes. Test for setting. Pot and cover. Makes about 8 lbs.

Jellied Beetroot

4 medium sliced beetroot | 1 cup clear vinegar
½ cup sugar | 1¼ packet gelatine
1 cup water |

Boil and prepare beetroot. Put into jars. Put vinegar, water and gelatine in a saucepan. Stir well and bring almost to the boil. Pour over earlier prepared beetroot.

Lemon Curd

1 lemon | 1 oz margarine
4 oz sugar | pinch of cornflour
1 egg |

Grate the lemon and squeeze the juice. Put in saucepan with the sugar, cornflour and margarine and add yolk of egg. Beat egg white stiffly and fold in. Cook over a gentle heat until boiling. Pot and cover.

Mixed Fruit Marmalade

2 large grapefruits	8 pints water
2 oranges	1½ lb sugar to every pint of pulp
2 lemons	

Wipe fruit and cut in two, extract juice keeping seeds in a small bowl. Cover these with ½ pint boiling water. Shred rind of fruit finely, put into large basin and cover with 8 pints of water. Allow to stand overnight, boil next day in a covered saucepan until rind is soft. Boil seeds for a few minutes and strain into pulp. Measure the liquid and to each pint add 1¼ lb sugar, warmed. Stir until sugar is dissolved and boil fast until it sets about 30-40 minutes.

Orange Marmalade

3 oranges, sieved	3 pints water
1 lemon	3 lb sugar

Boil oranges and lemon in 3 pints of water until soft, simmer for 1 hour. Cool, remove fruit. Chop and return to water. Add 3 lbs sugar and boil until it thickens. 1 tsp of tarlic acid helps to thicken.

Raspberry Jam

1 lb (450 g) fruit	1 lb (450 g) sugar

Clean fruit, grease saucepan with butter. Simmer raspberries for 10 minutes. Add sugar and simmer for a further 10 minutes. Pot and seal.

Tangarine Conserve *preserves for diabetic diet*

4-6 tangarines	½ grapefruit (total weight of 1½ lbs)
½ lemon	2½ pints water
1 level tsp tartaric acid	1¾ powdered gelatine
30-35 saccharine or other sweetening tablets	

Wash fruit, peel tangarines, cut peel into strips and tie in a muslin bag. Cut other fruit finely and add tangerine pulp to water and acid in pan. Bring to the boil and simmer gently till all fruit is tender. Remove bag after 30 minutes so that tangarine strips do not become mushy. Remove strips from bag, rinse gently in cold water and drain. Strain pulp through scaled jellybag. Return juice to clean pan, bring to the boil and add saccharine, strips of peel and dissolved gelatine. Bring just to boiling point then pour into clean warm jars and cover at once with porosan skins (wax paper discs sterilised as is given above)

Raspberry Or Strawberry Jam *preserves for diabetic diet*

3 lbs raspberries or strawberries
1 lemon

40-45 saccharine tablets or other sweetners
1 lt glycerine

For strawberry jam squeeze and strain the lemon juice over the prepared fruit, both sorts of jam. Now continue with the same method. Heat fruit gently and mash with a wooden spoon to extract juice and cook the fruit. Take a little of the juice and use it to dissolve the saccharine tablets, return the dissolved tablets to pan , add the glycerine and boil till the jam thickens. Pour into warm jars and cover in usual way.

Damson Jam *preserves for diabetic diet*

1½ lbs damsons
20-23 saccharine tablets

¾ oz powdered gelatine
¾ pint water

Wash and cook fruit in ½ pint water until soft and thick. Remove stones and add saccharine. Dissolve gelatine in remaining ¼ pint water. Add to pulp and mix thoroughly as the mixture is kept boiling gently. Pour into small clean, warm jars and cover at once with (porosan skins) waxed paper. Place jars on a wooden rack in a pan, cover with hot water bring to the boil and boil for 5 minutes.

Apple & Lemon Jam *preserves for diabetic diet*

Peel, core and slice 2 lbs apples. Grate rind of one lemon. Then boil with the apples in about ½ pint water. When the fruit is tender add 2 lbs sugar and boil up again like any other jam recipe. Just before the end of cooking time add the juice of the lemon.

Children's Treats

Toffee Apples

4 tblsp golden syrup

1 dsp vinegar

4 tblsp sugar

4 apples

Wipe apples and put on sticks. Grease baking tray. Boil syrup and sugar together until golden brown. Test by dropping a little toffee in cold water, if sets, it is ready. Remove from heat and add vinegar. Dip apples into toffee. Leave for 30 minutes to harden.

Chocolate Shake *(serves 4)*

2 heaped tsp drinking chocolate

4 heaped tblsp vanilla dairy ice cream

3 tblsp boiling water

1½ pints chilled milk

Mix drinking chocolate to smooth liquid with water. Whisk in milk and 1 tblsp ice cream. Divide remaining ice cream equally between tumblers. Fill with milk mixture and serve immediately.

Christmas Pudding For Children

1 lemon jelly

2 oz plain chocolate

1 tblsp chopped raisins

2 oz chopped dates

1 tblsp chopped nuts

1 dsp chopped cherries

Make jelly in usual way. Melt chocolate over hot water. When jelly is at setting point, stir in melted chocolate, fruit and nuts. Rinse an ordinary pudding basin with cold water. Pour in mixture and leave to set. Decorate with fresh cream if desired.